The Mag.net reader

Processual Publishing. Actual Gestures

edited by
Alessandro Ludovico,
Nat Muller

ISBN 13 978-1-906496-20-3

Publisher: OpenMute
English language editing: Nat Muller
Copy editing: Vicky Anning
Layout: Alessandro Ludovico
The cover layout has been in part generated with the N-Gen software.

Realised with the kind support of LabforCulture.org and Arteleku

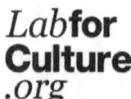 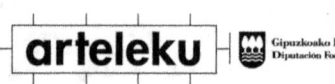

Contents.

Introduction.

Of Process and Gestures: A Publishing Act

Nat Muller and Alessandro Ludovico

Preceding the Act(ion)

The story starts like this: in July 2007 we organised a series of talks and debates for the *documenta 12 magazines* project on the topic of "Paper and Pixel". Not coincidentally, this was the subject of *The Mag.net Reader 2: Between Paper and Pixel*, which we had published earlier that year. As often happens with these events, it was after hours – between the lines, so to speak – that new alliances were forged, hot issues debated, and new projects cooked up. We did notwant this momentum to go to waste, and decided to capture in a new publication that moment of "ideas-in-the-making" that is so seminal to every editorial and publishing practice in a new publication.

Processual Publishing. Actual Gestures is thus in itself an act of making public what goes on behind the scenes. In this context we view the act of publishing as a gesture that accommodates the political, the artistic, and in some cases, the defiant. One might argue that we live in a day and age wherein gestures are not enough, and that only concrete action with a direct critique, aiming to instantly subvert and undermine, is the requisite strategy for expressing dissent. Yet, gestures are located between the realm of discourse and the material act. A gesture is something preceding the action, and therefore signifies motion and agency of the most expressive and potent kind, precisely because it is so wrought with intentionality. It is this sensibility that we would like to unfold over the following pages. This reader has been edited according to three main strands, which situate contemporary independent publishing as: a locus for artistic practice ("The Art of Publishing"); a public platform engaging with its readership in a specific manner ("Publishing the Public"); and a potential site for countering hegemonic informational power structures ("Hacktivist Publishing"). The thread stitching these realms together is the examination of conditions and tactics for the distribution of knowledge. We insist that the latter is by definition always work-in-progress, and in continuous active flux. For example, in "Manifesto for an Active Archive", the collectives Arteleku and Constant elaborate on their "Active Archive" project, which seeks participatory methods for the dissemination of content through digital cultural archives. Here the gesture is one of decentralisation, which transforms the collective sharing of resources into a surplus value for all parties involved.

The text is nicely juxtaposed with Pages' intervention, "Instances of a Purloined Voice", which questions the idea of central command and authenticity in regard to historical documents. Here the gesture seems to be one of caution, not only indicating that truth lies in the eye of the beholder, but also that ink on paper and voice on tape are not innocent media. In that sense, the purloined voice of the Shah during the 1979 Iranian revolution and the piecing together of the shredded archive of US embassy intelligence officials in Tehran mark a point of re-publication through a highly editorial process.

If publishing is a material act, then how to articulate its manifestations vis-à-vis institutional issues, and their respective relations to the public domain? Curator Jelena Vesic ponders the production of intellectual content – if not subjectivity of culture workers – in the contemporary art world, while taking her cue from Maurizio Lazzerato's definition of immaterial labour, and social network theory and experience. Following the idea that participation produces public spheres in relation to contemporary artistic practice, Jaime Iregui and Patricia Canetti & Leandro de Paula discuss models and conditions of artistic and critical production, respectively in Colombia [esferapública] and in Brazil [Canal Contemporâneo]. While Iregui offers a genealogy of art as a segment of the public sphere (and its eventual dissolution), first in more general terms then linking it to the Colombian context, both he and Canetti concede that the Internet has facilitated a platform for content and collaborative knowledge exchange that otherwise would have been quite difficult to establish, past the mesh of institutional, political, commercial and other constraints. Both stress the importance of an active community that is involved as an active public, safeguarding the "publicness" of their respective projects, and continuously – in progress and process – redefining what the public is, and could be.

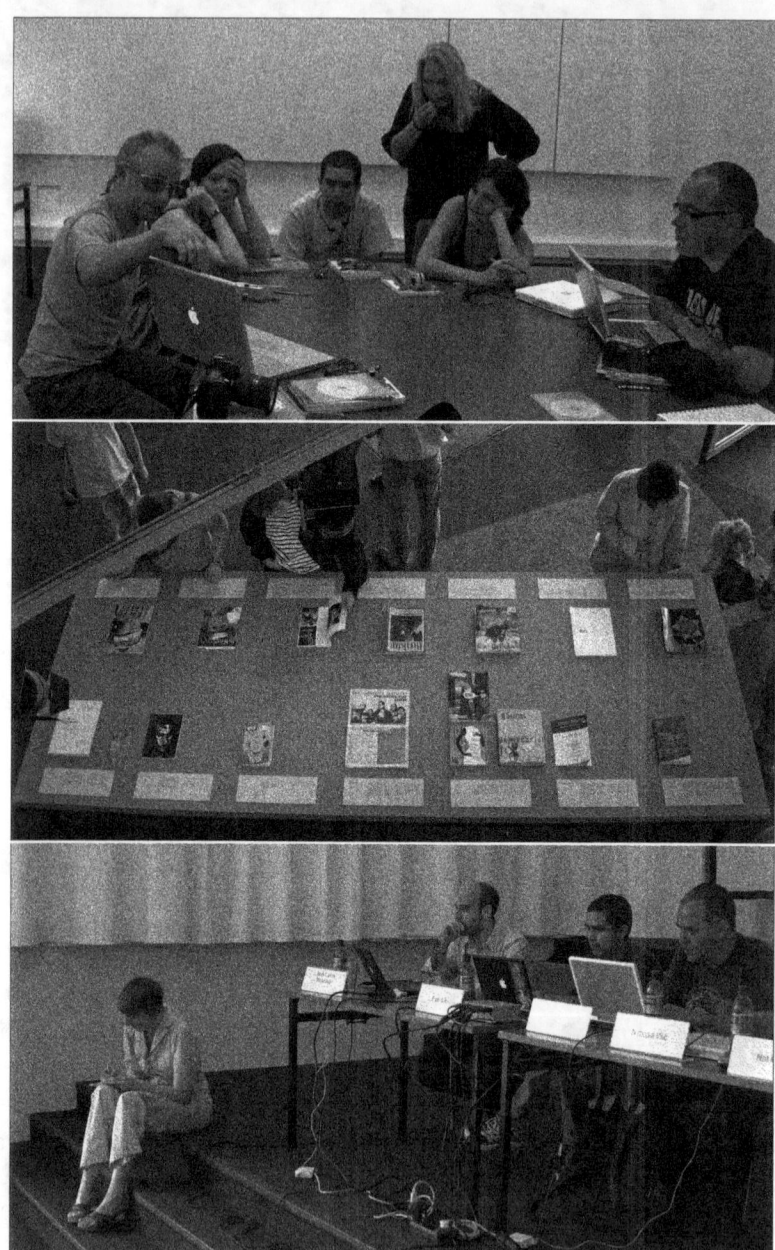

Social printing

The printed act's fragility is mirrored (more than simply caused) by the seemingly endless developments of online technologies. The unstoppable proliferation of online news, the first successful e-book reader (Amazon's "Kindle"), the rising cost of paper publishing, are all threatening the stability of print publishers, which are compelled to transform their business model into something new, yet hitherto unimagined. Chances of survival, and to continue to let the ink dry locally on cellulose (instead of simply temporarily switching the status of some magnetic storage somewhere in the world) remain uncertain. For example, the Amsterdam Weekly, a free English-language cultural newspaper from Amsterdam, recently launched an imaginative fundraising campaign: each of the upcoming content pages was divided into blocks and each block was sold for 5 Euros. Only sold blocks were printed, so if sales were disappointing, readers would receive a newspaper with blank blocks, devoid of content. This is an emblematic – perhaps even desperate – case of a social call-to-arms that would support a publisher in dire straits. Yet it underscores the unavoidable social role of the printed medium in a way that is quite different from the pre-programmed "social network" scheme. In fact, the former triggers a connection based on the shared interests between publisher and reader, while the latter is simply based on a (highly predictable) proximity between "content providers" and "6 degrees of separation" algorithms that connect people's abstract profiles data on similarity, leaving no room to randomness and complexity.

Print technologies are considered as subaltern by online aficionados, and are increasingly viewed as a mere tool. The IT industry propaganda feeds consumers with the usual fake – yet dazzling – creative genius lingo, which urges them to publish their own unreadable novel or childish poetry collections in cheap "few copies" editions. Or conversely, empty their bookshelves with an e-book reader, perhaps even compulsively print a disposable newspaper updated to the minute. After almost six centuries, print technology just cannot risk mutating into a giant abstract digital printer that can be used at will for online and digital content (just hit the metaphorical CTRL-P key!). Would this mean that print evolution is facing its final phase, and is slowly turning into an archival medium (like for example CD-Roms)? The latter would really mean its death, as a medium proper. Here, a radical change is to be detected between the lines: publishing on paper is not about rigorously selling and distributing content to a specific target readership. It is more a "gesture" that creates a space of intimacy between the publisher/editor and the reader. This space of intimacy is definitely a "physical" one.

That's why it is telling that the unchallenged Queen of Art Blogs, Regine Debatty, in her interview admits to being a heartfelt and passionate fan of print, whilst at the same time feels intimidated by the immutability of the medium. Debatty and her We-Make-Money-Not-Art blog are emblematic of the independent blogger, combining professional writing skills with an ethical, yet personal management of a successful online publishing platform, which has resulted in an enthusiastic international following. Her daily posts are only the most visible part of a process that involves an intricate weaving together of a vast personal network and different media.

This differs significantly from the dynamics of the mailing list as medium. The monthly curated threads on – empyre – manifest, as Christina McPhee points out, unique characteristics within a hectic online world, namely combining the relaxed pace of email postings with the unobtrusive aesthetic of the black and white text on screen. It is a choral dialogue in written form, designed by mutual gestures, involving specific topics, which become an unpredictable performance of readers and writers switching their roles continuously. The dialogue between Fran Ilich and his interviewer Cornelia Sollfrank, on the other hand, takes on a more classical form. Amongst Ilich's different publishing efforts, his hybrid sab0t pamphlet is a potentially revolutionary gesture: a pdf, easily downloaded from everywhere, and re-distributed in the Mexican streets with a literal gesture that pushes the content straight into the hands of the reader.

In his contribution "Ghosted Publics – the 'unacknowledged collective' in the contemporary transformation of the circulation of ideas", Andrew Murphie calls for a "horizontal life of the mind", which envelops the processual in publishing, and in social networks. His 23 theses are a base for a panoptic speculation on the nature of publishing and its new models, stemming in particular from a critique of academic models and its archaic paradigms. Murphie advocates for an approach where "publishing is no longer a question of 'readership', but of resonance".

If the most important challenge for print is to create an alternative and effective model of physical distribution within the chaotically connected infosphere, then Mute collective's latest project – NDS (Network Distribution System) – tackles that problem by proposing a spontaneous and distributed infrastructure to produce/sell/distribute independent cultural artefacts. NDS is the cherry-on-the-cake along an impressive amount of small Mute-developed cornerstone tools for the future of independent publishing. Mute has been at the forefront in designing prototypes for the ecology of editing and distributing information, and their networked practice contributes significantly to a better publishing world. The best metaphor for "content-in-the-making" is to be found in Miguel Carvalhais' graphic intervention, which is in and of itself an unveiled gesture: the preparation of a text. The bits of info stitching the written work together are represented as minimal digital windows, which are spread all over the visual space. The practices of copy/paste sampling and hyper-textual connecting tempt the reader to dip into an intimate involvement, highlighting the processual quality of publishing.

Finally, what we as editors of *Processual Publishing. Actual Gestures* wish to emphasise is that the printed medium still literary places the knowledge – if not the agency – in the physical hands of the reader. It is this gesture that we extend as an invitation, hoping that independent publishing continues its innovation and radical approach, and triggers a multitude of gestures, firing up a new underground wave of content, rippling the ocean of information.

The Art of Publishing.

Interview with Regine Debatty

Alessandro Ludovico

Alessandro Ludovico: I would say that we-make-money-not-art (wmmna) is a blog that expresses an impressive worldwide scattered community, part of the so-called "creative class", talking about art, design and technology – never forgetting an ethical, or sometimes explicitly political, approach. Do you acknowledge this definition? And when and why did you start?

Régine Debatty: Thanks for making clearer (even to me) what my blog is about. I would say that your definition is a perfect fit. The blog started in early 2004. It was just a place where I would collect everything I could find about something I knew very little about at the time: the intersection between art and technology. There was no strategy, no plan. It was nothing more than an archive of my findings. Very soon though I realized that I not only enjoyed learning about so many exciting practices and projects but also that the blog had aggregated an audience. It was gratifying and exhilarating. In the beginning though, wmmna was giving more coverage to gadgets and no-brain installations. As time passed, I found that the applications of technology were less relevant to my interests. I now focused more on artworks that reveal the implications of technology, be they cultural, ethical, social or even political.

A.L.: You told me that you're somehow worried by the idea of a wmmna printed anthology, mostly because print "cannot be corrected". How often do you correct blog entries? Conceptually what do you think of the printed medium?

R.D.: I actually almost never correct my entries but I like to know that I have the power to do it. Most of the time I would update a post because the artist whose work I was covering in the story asks me a few months after to put a more recent image or a link to a video of his or her work. I can't help feeling some sort of reverence for paper. I do know that not everything that is printed deserves to be given total credit and trust (it almost makes me cry to think of the trees, time and energy

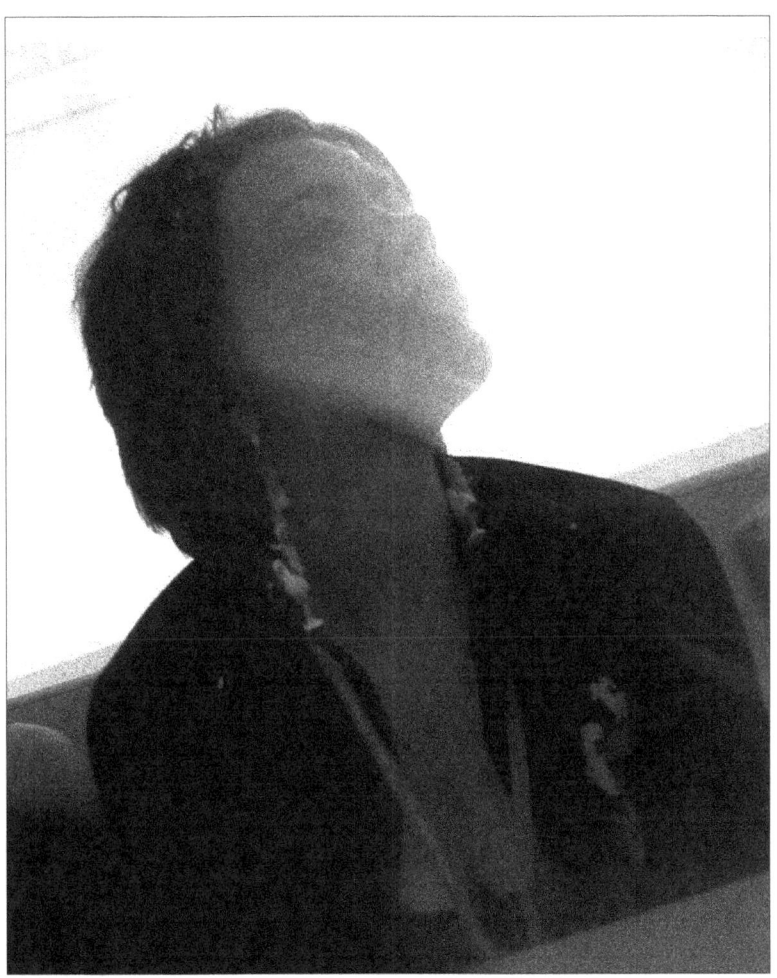

wasted on the so-called "gutter press") but I can't help it, I'm a paper fetishist. I don't think blogs could ever replace paper magazines but I can't live with only paper mags either. I need both. They are different and they fulfill different roles in my life. But maybe younger generations would think differently. There's the way one enjoys reading on a screen, vs in a book or magazine. I love writing in margins, marking corners of a book for interesting passages. I like reading an article while waiting for the bus. I like creative typography, beautiful images spread on two pages. I like touching the surface of the paper and smelling a new book as I open it.

And best of all, I can kill mosquitoes with magazines. You can do that with a laptop too of course but that's at your own risk. There's a different rhythm to paper. I write for paper magazines and I know that more than one month can pass between the moment you write a piece and the moment readers will be able to lay their eyes on it. So I will offer a different point of view for the magazine. I can't link directly to the website of the artists, or to new terms or events. I can't multiply the pictures that will illustrate my text in order to provide more context and details. And if my text is printed I feel responsible. There's a proof reader at the magazine but he can't beat the thousands of readers who will fire me a comment immediately, asking me to correct, develop or update a piece of information. I'm more careful when the printing is looming. There's also something about my own personality: I can't think in the long term. Printing an anthology would require some strategy and vision. I have neither of those, I'm afraid.

A.L.: In the wmmna evolution, you changed your blog form from a classic daily-post style, to longer, pondered and theme-related posts, often alternating them with reviews and interviews. Can you tell me how your editorial policy changed over time?

R.D.: It was quite natural. Just posting quick entries one after the other and adding a nice image is easy. Of course, it's better if you "curate" the flow of information to publish and choose the right mix of stories that will make your blog different from your neighbour's, but mostly, blogging is easy. Anyone can do it.
At some point it was just about finding a scoop, discovering the cool story before the others. That was kind of a no-brainer to me because I was already traveling a lot to see exhibitions and to meet many artists and designers. But after a year or two I also realized that what made my readers happy was to have my own take on a work or an event. It didn't matter anymore if I was there first. Besides, at some point I became dissatisfied and wanted to go deeper. I did not just want to write about an installation, I wanted its creator to give my readers more details about its motivations, the technical challenges he or she encountered while developing it, the way the public reacted to it when it was exhibited, etc. Same goes for the reviews of the exhibitions I see. Now I just take my time. Instead of writing a fast story, I contact curators to get a few words from them about their show, I look around and gather as much information as

possible before publishing anything, I also write to the press office to get pictures that are far better than the ones I can make. I still take pictures. First of all because the press office would never send me the image I dream of, the one from a particular perspective, the close-up on a detail I find meaningful, etc. Most of the time you have this gorgeous photography of an installation but without the public interacting with it, or from an angle no one would ever get to experience. The other reason why I take pictures is that I make them all available to the readers on flickr so they can choose which one deserves their attention: the swanky press picture or the so-so image I took of two kids laughing their heads off while playing with an interactive installation. Today my audience has changed along with my style and approach of course. Those who liked the gadgets and quick stories won't read me anymore but I gained others who appreciate the more in-depth coverage and the slow rhythm. I'm actually getting closer and closer to a magazine but I want to keep the personal and relaxed attitude of a blogger.

A.L.: Can you tell me more about how the advertisement for blogs works? Is it really the dominant funding model and are there any ad schemes or networks that are able to support the independent cultural blog scene?

R.D.: There's the almost inevitable Google adsense, which does not work for me at all. I have enough audience to make a decent living but I have the wrong content. I should write about mobile phones or microwave ovens. Because it is difficult to identify clearly the content of the blog, the ads I get most of the time are totally irrelevant and sometimes utterly ridiculous (I quite enjoy the former though, I've had ads for slaughterhouse materials, stuffed squids and Iranian carpets). I can now rely on this company (Federated Media), which finds advertisers for me, and that is extremely relaxing. They've basically allowed me to keep on working and living in good conditions. The only problem is that no one wants to put their ads on an art blog. So FM "sells" my blog as being part of a pool of "Graphic Design Blogs". I am actually very surprised to see that years are passing and advertisers are still sticking to the banners on the homepage model. 65% of my readers actually never see my homepage; they follow the stories everyday from the comfort of their rss reader. Two or three years ago I signed a deal with Feedburner so that they would handle ads in the feeds but the amount of money I make is as ridiculous as it was three years ago. They keep telling me that things will get better "soon". Right! It would make sense though. The audience is there en masse and the layout is perfect to ensure that readers can't miss the ads too (I think we've all trained our eyes not to see the ads that appear in the sidebar of the blogs).

A.L.: You told me that you are often faced with problems of getting press accreditation (even if wmmna is way more popular and focused than most of the usually accredited magazine/newspaper). Do you feel you are very different from a paper magazine? And do you notice a change in attitude lately, or do you think that it will take time to give bloggers the recognition they deserve?

R.D.: Oh yes! It is so different to be a blogger. I can't count anymore the times when I would arrive at the press accreditation booth and say I write on this blog called we-make-money-not-art, and they'll look at me with scorn in their eyes because bloggers don't count as press. No matter how careful you are in writing your review, no matter about the quantity and quality of the audience you have. Then I would add that I also have a column on a posh British art magazine and I'll get almost whatever I request. A few years ago, I asked for an accreditation to a key media art festival. I had been covering their festival for two years at least and I knew that most of the artists selected for the festival valued my review a lot more than they'd value an article in some non-specialist paper magazine. But the press office said no. I won't put the blame on the festival. They just had this external press office that had no idea of the relative importance of a niche blog like mine for the festival. So someone (well, it was you, Alessandro) stepped in and explained to the press lady why she might want to reconsider her decision. She did and now she makes sure I get a catalog and an invitation to all the art events she works for. She's actually a very smart and clever person and I'm glad I later got to meet her. The situation depends on the location. When I'm in New York, for example, I hardly ever face any opposition. Blogs are important; bloggers are part of the media scene. In Europe things are slower to move. Some countries are more open to blogs than others. It also depends on the age of the organizers, the young ones being more receptive. I've learned to live with that kind of situation too. If the press people won't let me in, I'll just lie. But most of the time, I pay my entry like anyone else. I'd rather do that than face the humiliation of looking like a cheap gal hunting for a freebie. And if I am not allowed to take pictures of the exhibition, I will do it anyway (unless I know for a fact that the artist doesn't want that or if the subject is a bit delicate) or I'll write one of the artists on show and they'll find a way to send me the press package. I'll do anything to write something complete and relevant for my readers to enjoy. On the other hand, I can also blame my own laziness: I should apply for a press card and I'll get free entrance to any museum or exhibition. I will get the nice CD with the press images (that's funny how many press offices will still mail you a CD instead of giving you a code that enables you to download the images immediately from a website) and I will get the respect from the press office employees, even if I were to write for a magazine specialized in coffins.

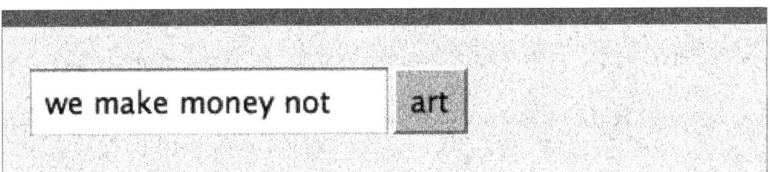

A.L.: Part of the academic world still snubs the blogosphere as inaccurate, arbitrary and with no control from peer reviewers. What's your relationship with academia?

R.D.: Well, I sometimes agree with those who claim that bloggers are inaccurate because some of them really are. I often give talks, and on several occasions some bloggers would attend my presentation and publish notes about it. Sometimes they are truthful to the spirit of my talk, but sometimes their notes are appalling: they put words and ideas in my mouth I totally disagree with. It is so embarrassing. But I have even worse stories to tell you about "professional" journalists and how they distort my words in order to get a more exciting story to publish. Most of the famous bloggers are conscientious and careful bloggers though, and there is something similar to peer reviews that ensures that they will do their job properly. First, there are the comments: if you write something even slightly inaccurate, there will always be someone out there to correct you. Two, you can feed your readers with lies every single day if you want. There's nothing that will prevent you from publishing them, but readers are not idiots either. If they find a lack of respect for truth or some half-cooked thinking on your posts, they will just stop visiting your blog. And without readers, a blogger is little more than a vox clamans in deserto. I don't have much relationship with academia. When some researcher or professor from a university of the arts or other computer-related department writes me it is usually to thank me for the information I provide their students with, or to invite me to give a talk in their class. Of course there are very probably some people from academia out there who would be relieved if bloggers like me could disappear from the surface of the web planet, but they usually won't email me to inform me of their thinking.

A.L.: Are Google-Technorati a dangerous duopoly in establishing the 'value' of a blog, respectively with the "page rank algorithm" and the "blog authority"? How do you manage it for your blog?

R.D.: Ah! Google! That one drives me crazy! I still can't grasp where the logic is in the way they handle page ranks. One day you do a search on a particular art genre and results from my blog will come high up the first page, sometimes they'd be buried somewhere in page 4 limbo. Then there are the many re-blogs that just copy and paste my posts. That's quite flattering but it's also a mixed blessing because most of the time, and no matter how obscure these re-blogs might be, they'll appear far above my original post on Google results. I learnt to live with that. There's nothing I can do about it I guess. I've stopped paying attention to Technorati for ages. I think many bloggers did the same. A few years ago, they put some really embarrassing and almost insulting advertising links among the results emerging from a search on my blog. I wrote them a kind letter asking them to do something about that, that there was some limits to greediness and that maybe it was not very professional to confuse their users with their way to display results. Nothing happened. I published a post to complain about it. Cory Doctorow kindly came to my rescue and wrote one of the top persons there, asking him to do something about the situation. The guy wrote me, saying he was sorry and he'd fix it, but he never did. Neither did he answer any further messages I sent him. So out Technorati! Their lack of respect for the community they thrive on has scandalized me beyond words.

A.L.: People usually tend to identify you with we-make-money-not-art. What are the main advantages and drawbacks of this specific condition? In your opinion, is it going to change in the near future, finally identifying the blog as a medium with a capital "M" or not?

R.D.: Yes, I often get that "Hello, are you we-make-money-not-art?" question. And in some way that's true: I am the blog. I try to keep a rather personal relationship with my readers, answering everyone (gosh! do I sound like Jennifer Lopez here?) or helping the students who would like to get my opinion about the school most adapted to their interests, or the book(s) to read on a particular subject. But most importantly it's easier to identify the blog with me, than with any peculiar topic. It's not a blog focused on a particular aspect of the art scene and even the several themes I explore vary over time according to my interests. Which sometimes creates some problems, as some artists and designers might resent the fact that most of my enthusiasm today goes to biotech art and activism, and not to interactive design or playful installations anymore. So I would often tell them that wmmna is not a democracy. It is no one's blog but mine. I set myself some limits though. I'm actually very passionate about beauty products but I'm not going to review my favourite triple oxygen face mask on wmmna. Actually when some editor asks me to write a column for their magazine, a chapter for a book, or a text for a catalog, that's always what they request: something intimate, laid-back and personal like my blog. They don't want the blogger's point of view, nor do they want the expert's. What they ask for is the point of view of the expert who also happens to be a blogger. I think the blog is a medium. I don't see anything beyond a technical application that makes publishing fast and easy. And like any medium there are some gems, there is some trash, but you quickly learn to distinguish one from the other.

Processual Editing and -empyre-
Soft-Skinned Space: a Personal Account

Christina McPhee

-empyre- is a process-based listserv on media art and culture founded in 2002 by Melinda Rackham, based in Sydney and hosted at the College of Fine Arts, University of New South Wales. I came upon it accidentally when I read about Melinda's net.art work Contagion in the online magazine chairetmetal (metal and flesh), edited by Canadian media theorist Ollivier Dyens. He had also selected one of my projects, Slipstreamandromeda, for the same issue.

Melinda was starting -empyre- just then, as an extension of the trope of contagion/infection: provocatively, she called it a 'soft-skinned space'. I signed up, and joined the conversation with Melinda's first guest, none other than Ollivier, who had just published Metal and Flesh with MIT Press in 2001. Ollivier and Melinda's shared fascination with the imaginative connotations of 'contagion' appealed to my sense of irony and adventure in equal doses. At first, I imagined the -empyrean- as a mutation of the Yellow Submarine, possibly carrying on board some weird, oddly pleasant pathology, or media path-lab. Melinda spoke of her utopian hopes for -empyre-, as it might develop a non-hierarchical, open forum outside the usual conventions of academia and the art world. Even the name declined to be capitalised, implying a delicious subvention of Empire into the empyrean.

In the coming months, - empyre- proved to be a way to learn almost effortlessly about what was quickly developing into the contentious field some called 'new media'. Fuelled with a hopeful optimistic energy, -empyre-'s almost casual, self-effacing style (Melinda in those early days refused to even sign her name to her moderating posts) was most infectious, and grew rapidly. Our readers started in the south, but soon the list had moved beyond Oz and the Kiwis, while still retaining the laconic pithy tone of Down Under sensibilities. Soon -empyre- attracted other moderators, usually from the Americas or the Pacific Rim[1]. Each month a new topic would launch with a question or thematic focus. As moderators we would identify themes and provocative questions, and then contact

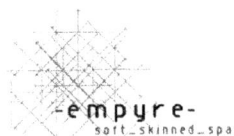

-empyre-
soft_skinned_space

-- about --- guests + topics --- joining + using --- archives + search --- who is --

About -empyre-

-empyre- facilitates critical perspectives on contemporary cross-disciplinary issues, practices and events in networked media by inviting guests -key new media artists, curators, theorists, producers and others to participate in thematic discussions.

-empyre- is an Australian based global community which preserves its autonomy as a non-hierarchical collaborative entity by engaging with new content on a monthly basis. The list was instigated by Melinda Rackham (AU) in 2002. The community grew exponentially and within the first year Adrian Miles (AU) and Rebecca Cannon (AU) joined briefly as facilitators. Long-term facilitators Christina McPhee (USA) and Michael Arnold Mages (USA) were invited to the -empyre- curatorium soon after, and during the next years they were joined by Jim Andrews (CA)and Felix Sattler (AU/GER). In 2005 Tracey Meziane (AU) and Marcus Bastos (BR) joined the team, and in 2006 and 2007 it was extended with Sérgio Basbaum (BR), Nicholas Ruiz III (USA), Renate Ferro (USA) and Tim Murray (USA). To find out more go to who is -empyre-

-empyre- global community conducted three moderated conversations in 2006 and 2007 on the three leitmotifs of documenta 12, as part of the documenta 12 Magazine Project. The list discussions: Is Modernity our Antiquity?; Bare Life; and What is to be done (education)? are produced and edited by Christina McPhee. Links to the discussions and edited essays are available for download here.

-empyre- often collaborates with institutions and festivals to produce dynamic online forums for physically located events. One such collaboration with Cornerhouse in Manchester, has produced a freeware Reader on 3d art and games which can be downloaded here. In addition -empyre- participates in other projects: here is Marcos Weskamp's Social Circles visualization time slice of the list dynamics.

-empyre- is currently archived by Pandora, a project of the National Library of Australia, dedicated to preserving online publications of national significance for future generations, and by the Rose Goldsen Archive of New Media at Cornell University, as a repository of emergent ideas amongst those working at the leading edge of contemporary practice.

-empyre- is not a chat space, nor an announcement or self promotion list, nor online performance space, and doesn't accept HTML formatted email or attachments on the list. The facilitators reserve the right to not publish posts that disregard these guidelines, or the current month's topics, disrespect the featured guests, or monopolize the forum either via individuals or group, and may unsubscribe anyone consistently doing so.

To join **-empyre-** or to change your subscription options go to joining + using.

-empyre- Facilitators

-empyre- list facilitators can be reached by mailing here
-empyre- face by u:sun
-empyre- site maintained by melinda rackham
-empyre- server upkeep by nigel kersten

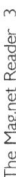

artists, theorists, curators, media journalists and others, weeks in advance of the topic's launch. Our guests would command a broad range of practices, from critical theory to computational poetics, from political hacktivism to industrial design.

It was the mix that counted, and still does, as we've found that the best way to keep the flow going is to pick a broad topic or question, to which we ask the guests to write specific responses and provocations. We ask each of our four to six guests per month to prepare an opening statement or query in short form. This way, the formal character of the topic – its writerly exposition – is evident from the start. The -empyrean- readers react, respond and riff from here. Guests stay 'on' for a negotiated period, from one week to the full four weeks. Posts are usually in English but sometimes also in Spanish, French and Portuguese. Readers and moderators contribute translations as needed. The shared editing/contributing becomes collaborative hypertext, almost a literary work through this collective process, and generates an archive of new media thought and production (now in the collections of Cornell University Libraries/Rose Goldsen Archive of New Media Art and with the Pandora Archive, National Library of Australia.)

Participation occurs both through the 'algorithms' set up by the guests as they put content out into the list milieu, and by the semi-random commentary and reaction on the part of the readers. You never know who among the readers will get fired up and start writing seriously, upping the ante on the official guests of the month. You never know when the list will go from mix to remix, from a simple set of themes to a fugue state. I find this exciting: if the -empyrean- implies a space of x, in the heights of the sky, then here we discover the unpredictable moves of communally generated narrative by multiple authors They all have a stake in making the story interesting and they aren't bound by any format other than the announced thematic, while possible transformations of the theme occur across a triple register of moderation, guest posts, and reader posts. The triplet structure maintains -empyre-'s unique dynamic as an open form.

As a moderator, I soon realise that I am deep into a kind of processual and collaborative editing, in which the readers become writerly and vice versa. Here guests and readers alike start to perform a special kind of tactical writing together – "call and response" in waves. The guests have a privileged voice-space: they can write in the vanguard of everyone else. At the same time they have the obligation to respond, not to drop out or disappear during the time of engagement with the -empyrean- readers, who may as quickly turn into writers as consistent and trenchant as any of the guests. Among the special guests, this dynamic of obligation 'lite' – a sort of volunteer slavery to the list for a short time – brings out competition and generosity in equal measure. In the realm of the readers, there is attentiveness in free flow, like a background hum of thinking going on through multiple time zones.

I've been interested in the remix like everybody else in new media. But it seems important to try to do something beyond just recontextualising information. There is no dearth of opportunities for communicating online. It's really about what makes people want to contribute, to write, even formally, or more conversationally, in an open self-generative work that still stays somehow grounded. It seems crucial to get past the tyranny of presets in digital media, the multiple choice aspect of everything Web 2.0. And so the leanest most minimal structure, or rules of the game, seem delightful and even fanciful. If there is not a 'formatting' issue or a cgi interface for selection among predetermined choices, will people want to play? So the crux of -empyre- has until now been non-visual, focused on the word, on a sort of expanded – even trippy – aesthetic of letter-writing. It's so old school it's almost Jane Austen.

Much virtual ink is bled over the problem of how to establish trans-border dialogues, how to create a public 'heterotopia'. This is a desire with more than political and aesthetic overtones. Indeed it reaches into the realm of magical thinking, as if we might overcome loneliness, isolation, and distraction by the strange harmonics of a conversation through as archaic and non-visual a medium as the lowly email. Or they may be the symptoms of an incipient delirium – a fever of desire for some harmonics across a spectrum of human speech, far wider than the normal audible range of the internet. Wider in the sense not of bandwidth, but of the human spirit. I hope for a kind of expansive mood of play to take hold amongst this self- selected, mostly silent group of a thousand readers/writers. For me, as artist and editor, this hope carries out through seduction and juxtaposition. I try to entice special guests to give of their time and to meet and respond to other guests whom they probably do not know personally, or have never met, and who are not necessarily likely to share a common argot. I remind them to post often, with generosity, and without expectation of response from the elusive -empyrean-readership, whose silence is the norm. The silence is a kind of nurturing presence: you get the feeling, when you write on -empyre-, that many are paying close attention, or that perhaps your thoughts are winging into their drifts as they access email on high speed bullet trains via blackberries and pods. Or there is another kind of space on -empyre- at times, a not-silent ricochet space, like a handball court where furious volleys rebound and strike. -empyre- is not a space of understanding, it does not explain itself. It does not require cooperation nor endorse neutrality. Posts, like hard balls at high speeds, smash at each other. Often on my watch this condition of almost violent play erupts unexpectedly. There will have been long silences on the list, practically nothing happening, and then someone takes up the game.

I've been thinking a lot about Ant Farm lately. This late sixties/seventies subversive architecture group was a self-described 'art politics'. Asked to comment on 'Media Burn', an installation in which Ant Farm members drove through a wall of flaming televisions using only a video camera mounted on the back of the car hood for guidance through the flames, one Ant Farm member ('Uncle Buddy') responded with reference to a kind of detournement of cars and televisions into a (literally) explosive transposition. "The idea of looping back into television is the destruction of television." [2] Ant Farm wanted to break up the hegemony of television by symbolically 'using' stacked televisions and flaming in order to release video for provocative deployment, beyond what they saw as the malevolent reach of capitalist media. Might -empyre- want to figure out a way to create/perform some kind of 'media burn' on the aesthetics of Web 2.0,? Web 2.0 and television are alike in the sense that both seem to promise a total hegemonic space, a 'ritual pathos' for everybody (the description is Ant Farm's). If Web 2.0 is unlike TV, as it makes possibilities for inclusion, remix and gift exchange, do we still need to 'burn the TV' by driving 'blind' (since -empyre- uses only hypertext, no images)? If we adopt Web 2.0 styles, do we lose the power of literary and political rhetoric, especially satire and polemic? Can we figure out how to perform a latter-day 'media burn'?

Notes

[1] More on -empyre-'s mechanics, simple rules of the game, and past and current glories, searchably archived and otherwise, are online at http://subtle.net/empyre. The list is currently moderated by Melinda Rackham (AU), Nicholas Ruiz III (US), Christina McPhee (US), Marcus Bastos (BR), Jason Nelson (AU), Renate Ferro (US) and Tim Murray (US)

[2] The quotes from 'Uncle Buddy' on Media Burn and context on Ant Farm are from Felicity Scott's new book, Architecture or Technoutopia, Chapter 8, "Shouting Apocalypse," p. 138. Cambridge: MIT Press, 2007.

Manifesto for an Active Archive

Arteleku-Constant: Miren Eraso, Nicolas Malevé, Laurence Rassel, Femke Snelting, Maider Zilbeti

This Manifesto is a work in progress. The text introduces the ideas and motivations behind the Active Archives project initiated in 2006, led by Constant in collaboration with Arteleku. The latter aims to create a free software platform in order to connect a plethora of practices: from the library to the mediatheque, from print publications (as magazines, books, catalogues), to productions of audio-visual material, events, and to workshops, discursive productions, etc. It accommodates practices that can take place online, or in different geographical locations, and which can be at various levels of visibility due to access rights, research disclosures, or privacy issues. The project takes course and develops throughout 2008-2009, and features regular workshops and public conferences in order to stimulate dialogue between future users, developers, cultural workers and researchers. *http://www.constantvzw.org/active_archive*

Creating web pages and displaying information online has become easier and easier for non-expert users. The Active Archives project starts from the observation that most of the interesting cultural archives that have been developed over the last few years have taken advantage of those new facilities for instant publishing, but mostly in the form of websites that mirror regular information brochures, announcements and text-publishing. Often, they are conceived as "We" give information to "You". Within Active Archives, we aim to set up multi-directional communication channels, and are interested in making information circulate back and forth. We would like to give material away and receive it transformed: enriched by different connections, contexts and contradictions.

Decentralizing the archive

When we want to share with other cultural associations and groups/institutions, the challenge is as follows: how do "We" share infor-

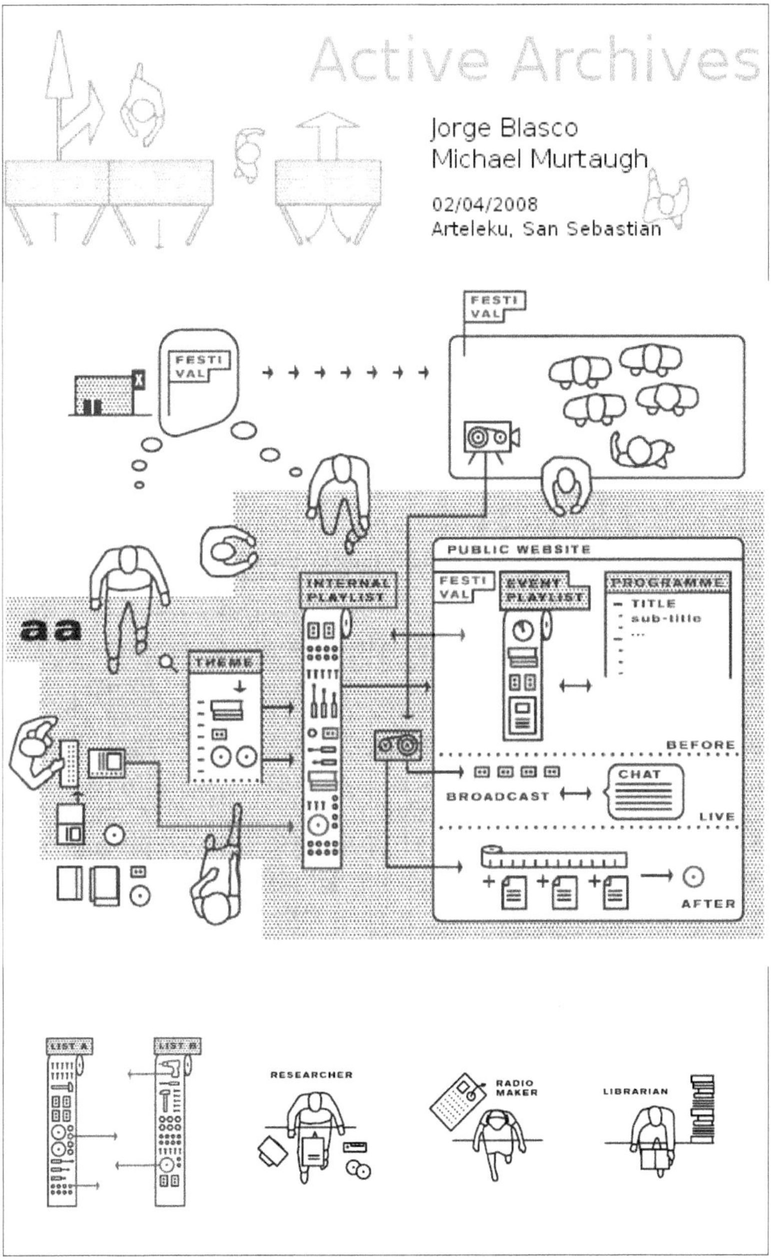

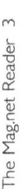

mation "Together". How do we channel information through each others' network, under which conditions? How do we produce digital content together? To develop common infrastructures, we will need to discuss what kind of licensing we prefer, and work on norms and a common agreement on formats. We also need to find a shared understanding of classifications or maybe first question existing ones.

Digital cultural archives today fall into two categories: fragmented archives and over-centralised archives. Fragmented archives look like isolated islands. Every institution sits on top of its treasure and tries to regulate and control the way it is used with at most offering a timid RSS feed. Centralised archives gather collections and resources from different origins but disconnect the material from its original context. Accessibility and searchability come at the cost of legitimisation.

An active archive is a decentralised archive that is not only open for reading, but also for re-appropriation, comment, divergences, transformations. This manifesto is a plea for such a decentralised archive: an archive constituted from many sites and voices that keep their own contexts without fear of sharing, mirroring, connecting and using common protocols.

Owning our infrastructure

If public television channels decide to publish their archives on YouTube, libraries work in partnership with Google etc., why does the Active Archive not make use of the existing Web 2.0 infrastructure? Flickr + MySpace + FaceBook with a bit of del.icio.us to glue it all together ... who needs more? But to upload digital culture on the servers of dotcom billionaires might not be such a good idea after all. However much influence the functionalities of Web 2.0 had in popularising the digital archive, we need to be aware of their terms of use. We would like to prevent that cultural archives serve as footage for ad-placement or as a honey pot for market profilers, and for this reason we need to make the effort to build our own infrastructure.

An active archive should provide to its contributors a clean and clear contract where the terms of participation are fair and legible for everyone. The goal of an active archive is to produce more interesting content in the first place. Not to make profit in monitoring the users and selling their behavioural patterns. Only when the different parties involved own their own infrastructure, and accept to share it, can they ensure the conditions for access without strings attached. This means open content

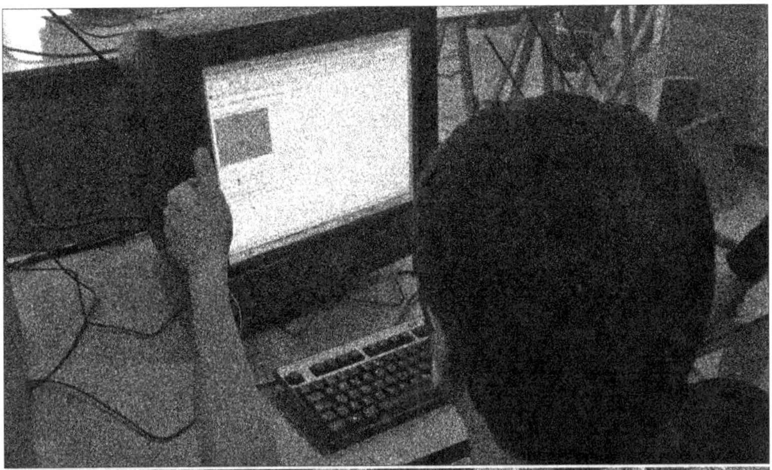

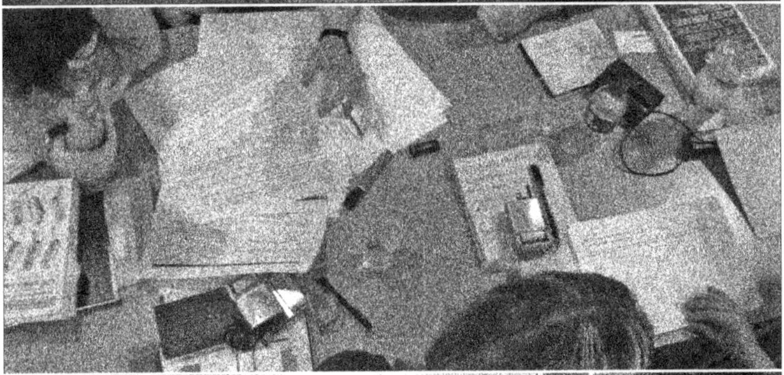

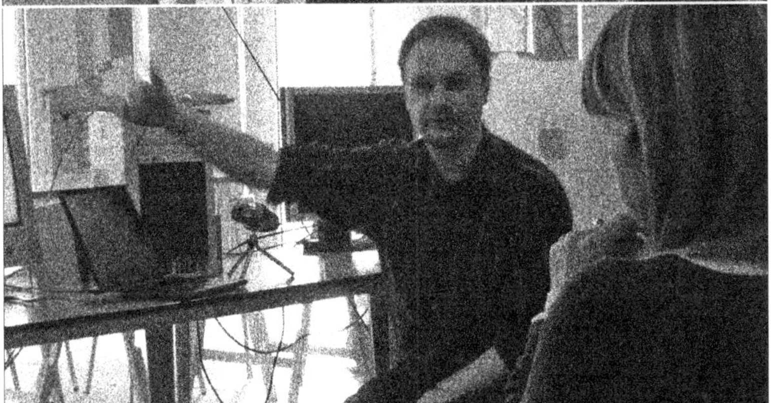

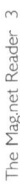

licenses for all material stored, so that the conditions for use are clear for everyone. An infrastructure built with free software so that everybody can co-own the source code.

Distributing more than text

An active archive needs to go beyond mere text-publishing. Artists, cultural groups and institutions regularly produce video and audio images for various communication or creative purposes. It is necessary to take into account that media content requires different material configurations: they need more disk space and more bandwidth, therefore they require clever strategies of distribution. Peer-to-peer networks have pioneered large-scale experiments with the distribution of audiovisual media, and it is time to learn from them.

Integrating audiovisual media is not just adding another type of file. It requires a new approach to navigation, searching, linking, subtitling and translation so that audio and video content can connect to text-based content. Otherwise those files remain black holes in the archives.

Promoting re-use

The material that is made available through the Active Archive is thought of as source material for other works. This means, systems need to be put into place to make referencing and re-use of the material easy, but also to make sure that versions of the material can filter back to the place its original came from. These systems are partially technical, and partially cultural: a series of commissions, workshops, exhibitions and publications will inspire creative use.

Between tags and ontologies

To improve the search facilities, to group elements together, to link them and to create new meaning and new experiences, an archive needs a system of classification. Librarians and archivists are used to work with fixed standards, but the work produced and discussed within contemporary culture tends to escape these classification schemes.

An Active Archive requires the creation and discussion of vocabularies and taxonomies that can evolve, diverge or merge. These vocabularies and taxonomies should neither be brutally top-down or completely flat. The system should stimulate the sharing of common classifications, allow for divergence, and promote the convergence of knowledge trees. An Active Archive needs a classification system with a difference.

Moving through new gestures

Sharing is the principal motivation to create an Active Archive. This means that we need to update our assumptions about the users of such an archive, the sources that are used, and the circulation of its content. An Active Archive is not a black box with a download button. It is information reconfigured. And it has to start now.

Instance of a *purloined* voice
Nasrin Tabatabai & Babak Afrassiabi

During the years before the 1979 revolution in
Iran cassette tapes were an important means for
underground circulation of oppositional voices
among the public.

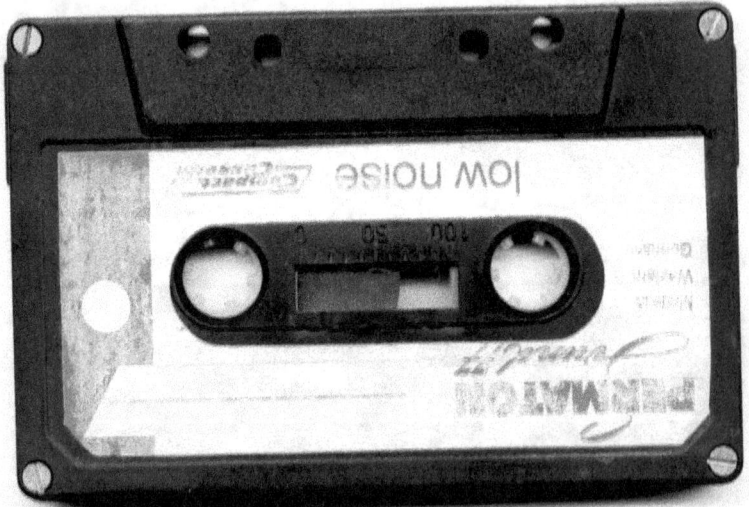

In the months leading to the victory of the revolution, select tapes were played back in public
rallies by holding a PA microphone close to the
portable tape-recorder. Other portable recorders
were often at hand for immediate duplication,
live mixed with the sound of the public.

In autumn of 1978 a tape-recorded message, pur-
ported to be the voice of the Shah, found its
way into the streets of Tehran. It was instruct-
ing the army of how to deal with revolutionary
mob and commanding them to shoot to kill.

Later the famous voice impersonator and come-
dian, Abdolkarim Esfahani, claimed to have re-
corded the tape in order to "shock the army and
politicize the movement."

The message on the tape was nevertheless what
people wished to hear because it fitted with what
they wanted to believe.

The impersonated voice
on the tape was never
a real voice since it
was fully destined by
what the public wanted
to hear. If it were a
recording of its true
owner, would the voice
have had a different
destination?

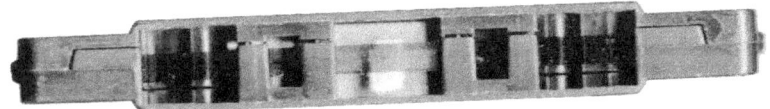

the always *purloined* voice

Instance of *purloined* pages
Nasrin Tabatabai & Babak Afrassiabi

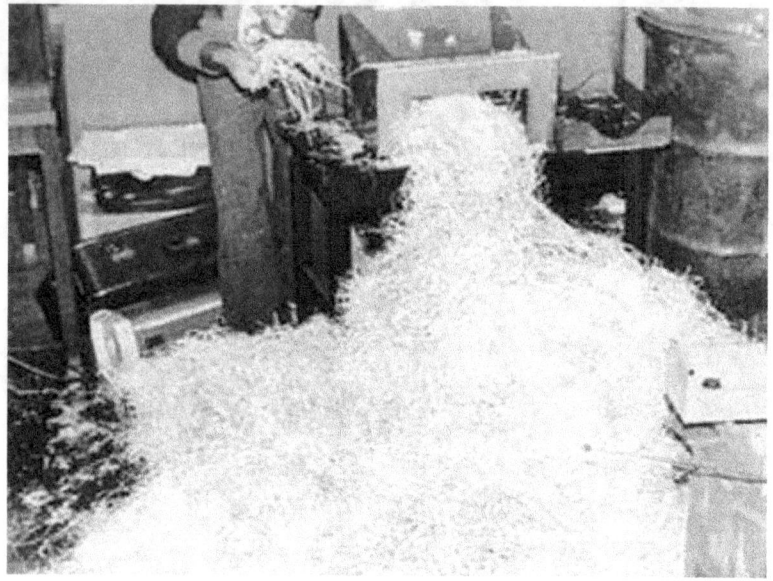

Iranian students having seized the US Embassy in
Tehran - November 4th 1979.

The US intelligence officials inside the Embassy
rapidly shredded confidential documents as the
buildings were being occupied. Many of these
documents were painstakingly reconstructed and
later published in several volumes to reveal US'
long-time political interferences in the country.

With the rejoining of corresponding shreds whole
pages were reconstructed to restore the *truth*.

restoring the letters or reassembling the slits?

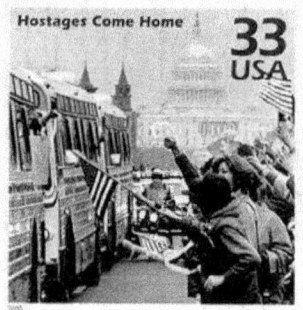

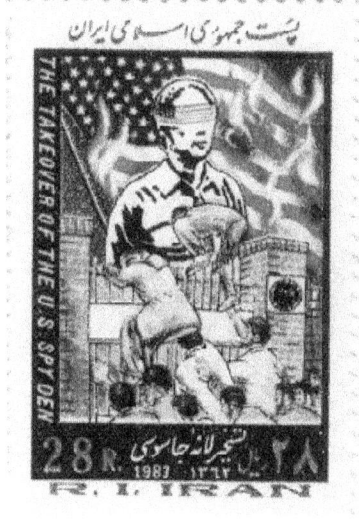

'The Takeover of The US Spy Den', Islamic Republic of Iran Post Company, 1983

Publishing the Public

The Spheres of the Public

Jaime Iregui

The public and the public sphere are concepts which contain a number of simultaneous meanings and that are defined self-reflexively. The public sphere has to do with what is common, with the state, with shared interest, with what is accessible. There is a historical mobility in the public-private opposition, which comes precisely from the mobility of publics and their forms of self-organisation. The public has a double meaning of social totality and specific audiences. The central idea is that publics are elusive forms of social groupings articulated reflexively around specific discourses.
Jorge Ribalta[1]

In an era when the privatisation of the public space is a generalised fact, it is necessary to wonder about the state of the *public sphere*, which since the early 20th century has lost its homogeneous character and has been transforming into an increasingly differentiated and diverse dimension, composed of a great variety of *spheres of the public*.

In *The Structural Transformation of the Public Sphere*[2], Jürgen Habermas defines the notion of public sphere as *an open ambit of debate where citizens deliberate over matters of common interest*. In the case of the *art world*, this would take place in cafes and halls as spaces for meeting and conversation, museums, opinion in the mass media, critical journals and exhibition and discussion spaces.

Habermas' abstract and idealised version of the bourgeois public sphere, in which the deliberation of civil society has to reach consensuses that act as a political force to influence the institutions under debate, has been redefined in recent years by several writers, including the critic and curator Simon Sheikh[3]. He points out that, in understanding the contemporary artistic environment as a kind of public sphere, we must keep in mind that we are not exactly dealing with a homogeneous and consensual sphere, but rather a platform in which disagreement and conflict between distinct subjectivities, policies and economies prevail.

Therefore, we can ask ourselves: are cultural institutions spaces open to interlocution and debate? How far is the public cultural sphere affected by the flows of the market? Can discussions about the local artistic environment involve publics from other countries and contexts? Must these discussions take on a *didactic turn* in order to reach a "wider public"?

As a way of exploring these questions further – and not necessarily as a historical journey through the distinct modes of the public sphere – in this text I am interested in focusing on a set of situations that reveal distinct forms of assuming and articulating spheres of the public from the art environment in Colombia.

In the public domain

Since the 19th century, the museum of art has been a fundamental part of the public sphere, insofar as it conserves and unfolds a set of aesthetic manifestations, which in turn produce a series of interpretations, opinions, postures, theories and debates.

The first half of the 20th century saw the emergence – first in New York and later in almost all the major cities of Europe and America – of a new kind of museum that operates as a space of representation of the experimental proposals of the avant-gardists: the museum of modern art.

In the first decades of its operation, the museum of modern art represented a utopian and experimental space; a laboratory of thought and

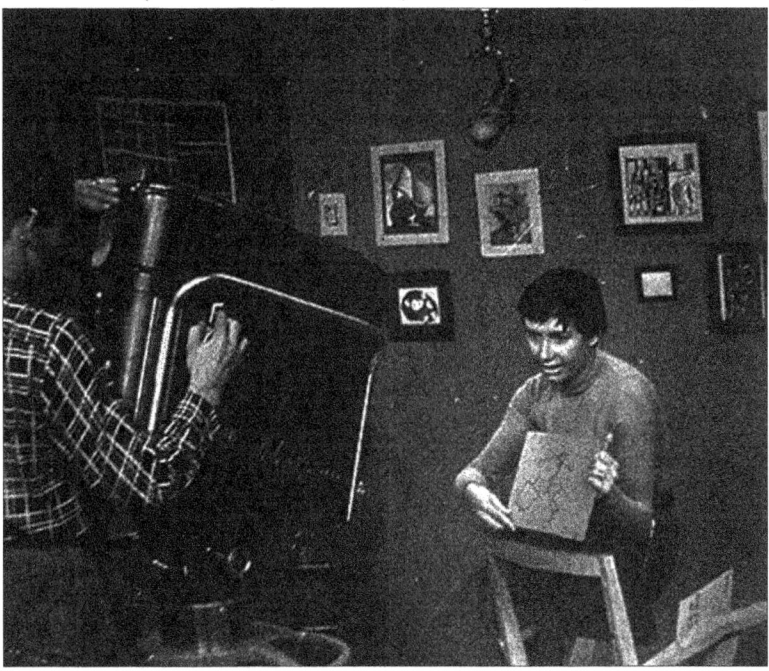

picture 1: Marta Traba

action; an independent and progressive space.

Gradually, this model became *established* along with its critical and museological purpose. Both the museums of modern art founded in different cities of the world and the commercial galleries dedicated to the promotion and sale of this kind of art took this exhibition model from the terrain of experimentation and risk to that of rampant institutionalisation. From this the museum emerged radiant as a spatial experience, where the collection loses its heritage character and transforms into a *cultural asset*, the edifice of the museum into artistic object and the public into a tourist-consumer.

In picture I we see the art critic Marta Traba in one of the first television programmes shown in Colombia. It was 1957 and this Argentinian based in Bogotá was determined to introduce the works and ideals of modern art into a fairly conservative society, for which art had to faithfully follow the principles of a representation whose reference was the late 19th and early 20th century avant-gardes.

Marta Traba is holding a map of Europe, which she possibly uses to show the countries from which modern art initially emerged. Behind her, on the wall, some reproductions of works by avant-garde artists can be seen. In front is the camera, which is in fact the public that has to be reached, that has to be informed about the foundations of modern art.

In addition to this television programme, Marta Traba gave lectures in various cultural centres of the city, was professor of history of art at the Universidad de América and belonged to the group of people who founded the Museum of Modern Art in Bogotá.

That was the moment when it was still possible to talk about criticism that sought to express itself with the *general public*, a criticism with pedagogical ends that saw – in the new technology of television – the possibility of reaching a large audience that must be made to understand the need to *modernise*. They would do this by knowing the works and advances of this new art, which had some representatives in Colombia: as well as critics, architects and other sympathisers, the production of artists such as Alejandro Obregón, Marco Ospina, Edgar Negret and Fernando Botero.

In general terms, this is a modern public sphere in which the art debates are in tune with the discourses and transformations of a society that seeks a solution to the serious social and economic problems that the country is experiencing in the ideals of abstract and rational modernity – promoted both from art and from the state and the private field.

The dissolution of the public sphere

Throughout the last decade, a series of processes began to emerge in different parts of the world where the modes of understanding artistic practice itself and the way it relates with the distinct spheres of the public were being reconsidered.

Since the 1980s, the modification of states of things is no longer implemented consensually as was done, for example, with the foundation and setting up of the Museum of Modern Art. It is now implemented through the initiative of groups of artists who act in disaccord with a modern public sphere where the discussion has a reduced group of authorised interlocutors: museum directors, critics, specialist journals and the works, trends and schools of thought that are given special emphasis in national exhibitions and other institutional events.

The theoretician Reinaldo Laddaga[4] refers to these processes as *"projects owed to the initiatives of artists and writers who, in the name of the will to articulate the production of images, texts, sounds and the exploration of the ways of living together, renounce the production of works of art or the kind of rejection that materialised in the most common productions of the latest avant-gardes, in order to initiate or intensify processes of conversation (or improvisation) that involve other artists for long periods in defined spaces, where aesthetic production is associated with the deployment of organisations destined to modify states of things in one space or another, and point to the constitution of 'artificial forms of social life', experimental modes of coexistence."*

The notion of the artist as a producer of objects is reappraised: the *trade* as a "set of skills and talents" is also understood – as Marcel Duchamp did in his time – as a set of "practices" and "modes of operation". But more than a question of language and theoretical models, the fact is that the *emergent*, the *contextual* and the *relational* move towards kinds of collaborative practices that have some relationship with those produced with the avant-gardes, insofar as they produce micro public spheres articulated around aesthetic proposals, discourses and modes of reaching a public through exhibitions and dissemination.

In contrast to what happens in countries with strong economies, where being "independent" implies having access to a great variety of state and private resources, these projects have been maintained with the voluntary contributions of their members, sales of their works, sporadic state aid and the organisation of auctions and festivals.

In the case of Bogotá, there are several exhibition spaces *(Gaula, El parche, Espacio Vacío, Only, La rebeca)* that worked in this way and articulated concrete audiences and modes of operation, both in terms of the exhibition and reception and dissemination of their processes: the artists conceived specific projects for these places; the length of the exhibitions varied between one day and two or three weeks; and they were mostly publicised without the aid of the mass media, which led to the construction of specific audiences through parallel platforms of dissemination and discussion.

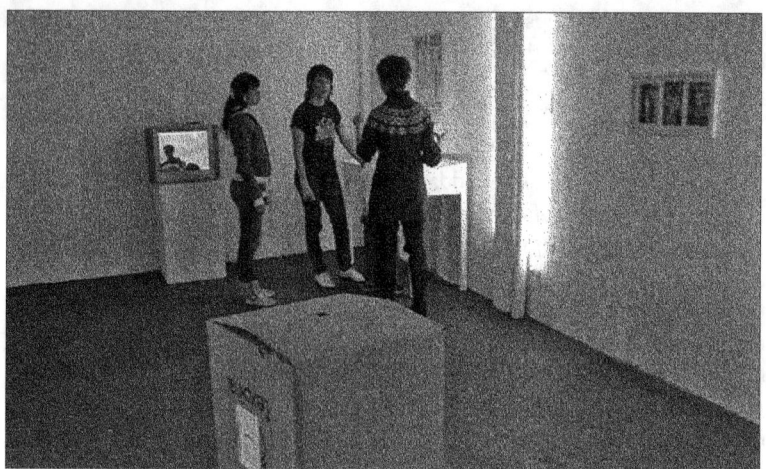

picture 2: Edwin Sánchez

In picture 2 we see a detail of the exhibition *Odio puro* by the artist Edwin Sánchez in *El Bodegón*[5], a space that *"emerged as a group initiative as a result of the absence of settings for the exhibition of alternative practices, projects by emerging artists and works with a critical aim. Its exhibition programme is focused on dialogue and the friction between diverse and, on many occasions, contradictory contents and processes. The internal structure of El Bodegón seeks to be horizontal and feed on dialogue and conflict. Halfway between the group of friends and the museum, it seeks to generate pedagogic processes around its own operation, based on the value of error and the awareness of failure. Its members are university students and professors."*[6]

Picture 3 shows a meeting of several artists from the city of Cali (Wilson Díaz, Ana María Millán, Beatriz Grau and Bernardo Ortiz) with the Brazilian curator Ana Paula Cohen in *Lugar a dudas*, an independent space which, at the initiative of the artist Oscar Muñoz, was opened in this city a couple of years ago and has become a place for reflection and

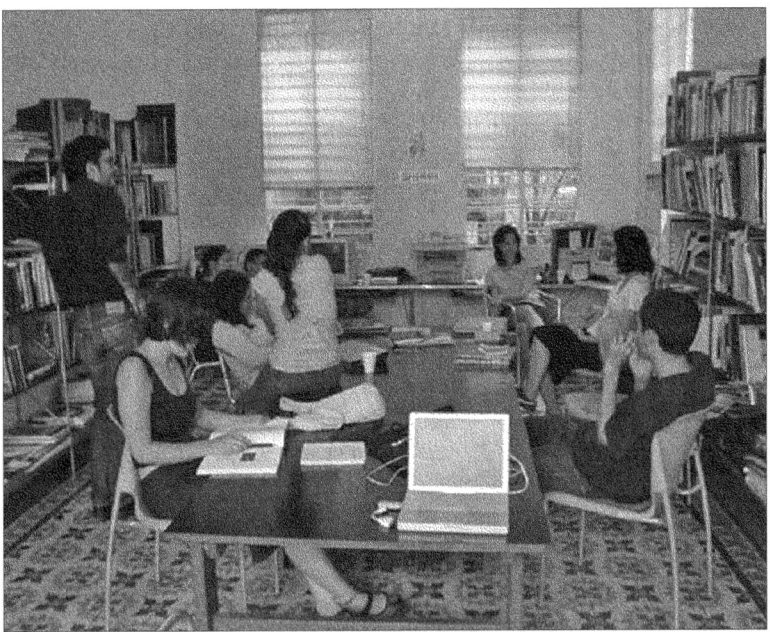

picture 3: Cali meeting

production of artistic thought through workshops, exhibitions, a residency programme, lectures and film seasons. It also has an excellent library and documentation centre supporting the research processes of students and artists.

Other projects *(Lugar a dudas, Festival del Performance, La rebeca)* have achieved the support of international institutions, which has not necessarily covered all the project management and running costs.

Although institutions such as the Ministry of Culture and the Secretariat for Culture, Leisure and Sport in Bogotá[7] have been adjusting their programmes of support and encouragement, in the case of exhibition proposals, almost all of them – except the curatorial grants for regional exhibitions – are oriented towards projects carried out in their exhibition spaces.

Networked islands

In the case of independent publishing projects, some began more than ten years ago[8], as in the case of the journal *Valdéz*[9], which is published *whenever it is ready* and achieves local or international support. *Hanguendo con patas* is a newspaper edited by the artist Raimond Chaves together with the residents of the Venecia[10] district in Bogotá. As well as working on the images, they participate with texts where they tell stories and anecdotes about the place. Other projects are more recent and are published and disseminated with their own resources, such as *Erguida*[11] and *NQS*[12], which publish one or two issues per year.

At the end of the last decade, various spaces appeared on the Internet characterised by their critical and deliberative attitude in terms of situations and issues that concern the artistic community[13].

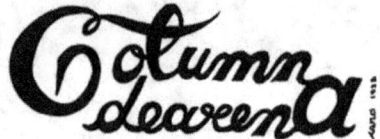

>> sobre Columna de Arena

José Roca
Reflexiones críticas
desde Colombia

José Roca es curador y crítico colombiano con formación en arquitectura, museología y crítica de arte (Whitney Independent Study Program, Critical Studies). Maneja desde 1994 las exposiciones temporales de la Biblioteca Luis Angel Arango en Bogotá. Forma parte de VOTI (The Union of the Imaginary), un foro online de discusión sobre práctica curatorial.

nuevo:
69 Extended Labels
   1 de junio de 2005

68 Sandra Bermúdez: mise en obs

67 agua como horizonte.
   Ana María Rueda

66 El Panóptico observado: notas
   Juan Fernando Herrán

65 Doubles Singuliers
   Ana Patricia Palacios

picture 4: Columna de Arena

In 1994, José Ignacio Roca was appointed Director of the Department of Visual Arts at Luís Ángel Arango Library, until then headed by the critic and curator Carolina Ponce de León. In addition to his tasks in this institution, he edited *Columna de Arena*[14], a space for criticism on the Internet where he periodically wrote about local and international exhibitions and events.

His columns differ from the type of criticism carried out by José Hernán Aguilar and Carolina Ponce until a few years ago, both because of the means used to disseminate it and the tone with which he begins and which is maintained throughout the process.

In his initial column, Roca introduces his proposal with these words: *"Faced with the absence of institutional spaces for publishing, there is another path for criticism: to generate its own spaces. In many countries the response of artists to the excessive rigidity of the institutional spaces has been the creation of spaces run by artists for artists; this strategy can work for criticism: a reflection on the artistic task that circulates, incestuously, between the world of art and those who gravitate around it, and which does not have the priority of reaching the 'general public'."*

[esferapública][15] was conceived from the outset as a space for discussion in which criticism is not necessarily taken as a value judgement on artistic events and objects, but as a space of reflection and exchange of opinion about situations and issues characteristic of the context of art.

This space operates as a self-organised forum: the discussions revolve around the issues that the members themselves propose and approach; among others, issues related to institutional practices, art criticism, curatorships, art and politics, artistic education and the state of the market. The different contributions offer diverse points of view about a problem and the aim is not necessarily to reach conclusions, consensus and implement solutions to the matters covered in the debates.

However, both the cultural institutions involved and those entities and/or people that bring about and are the object of the debates, assimilate – if they consider it pertinent – these reflections in accordance with their own criteria and possibilities of action: making the necessary adjustments in the case of an institutional practice, supporting or reconsidering a curatorial practice, adopting a position – public or private – on a matter under discussion.

Moreover, artists and critics edit blogs where they publish texts they have written for other media, as in the case of Emciblog by Mauricio Cruz, who occasionally adds updates, links, derivations and annexes. Ricardo Arcos Palma edits Vistazos críticos, which has its own distribution list, and Lolita Franco periodically writes about exhibitions and other events at a local level.

Spaces are also created for texts that have circulated through [esferapública], complemented by others produced specifically for these blogs: Catalina Vaughan adds links to articles and documents of reference; in Teatro Crítico Pablo Batelli creates a special index to look through his transcriptions of the media and television; Pedro Falguer edits an independent archive of his contributions; Carlos Salazar provides links to his texts with his photographs and Dimo García publishes texts and reports

The Mag.net Reader 3

of his everyday life in <u>Apuntes críticos</u>.

Is the map the territory?

Just as the experimental proposals of the avant-gardes were the starting point for producing a museum of modern art that in its early days was experimental, the artistic practices of the last decade that involved exhibition and publishing projects are the reference for a type of institutional self-criticism known as *new institutionalism*[16]. In other words, the appropriation – by a new generation of *progressive* curators, critics and cultural managers who work in museums, art centres and biennales – of large exhibition projects for kinds of *experimental* curatorships and flexible modes of operation (<u>Palais de Tokyo</u>, <u>Baltic</u>, etc.) and new kinds of spaces of sociability (<u>Rooseum</u>[17]), which are part *academia*, part *laboratory* and part *community centre*.

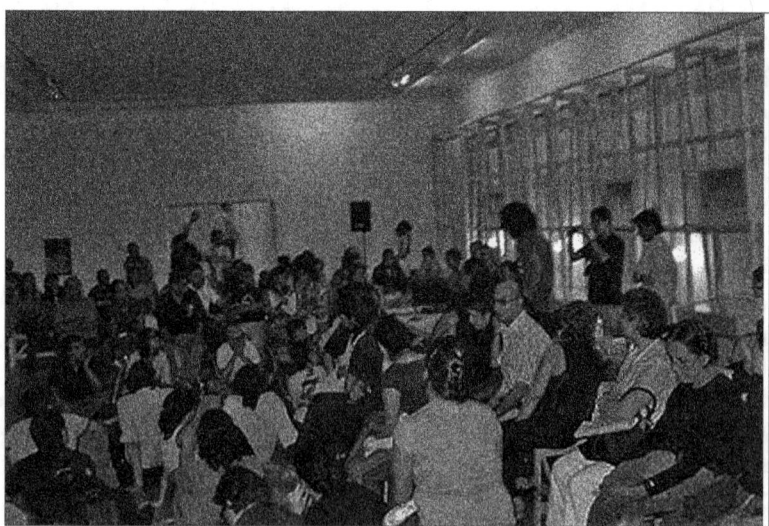

picture 5: Encuentro de Medellín 07

In picture 5 we can see one of the informal discussions that characterised the *Encuentro de Medellín 07*, whose main issue was hospitality, according to its curatorial team [17], as *"the temporary capacity of a space, whether physical, discursive or political, to host others and allow them to set out their interests and positions."* Artists were invited but it also had the participation of several independent spaces (*Capacete, La culpable, La jíkara, El*

Basilisco, El Bodegón, Helena producciones) and publishing projects such as *Valdez* and *Asterisco*.

The meeting proposed, in curatorial and exhibition terms, a critical revision of the model of the International Biennale held in the city of Medellín some decades ago. Instead of a sporadic macro-exhibition, a

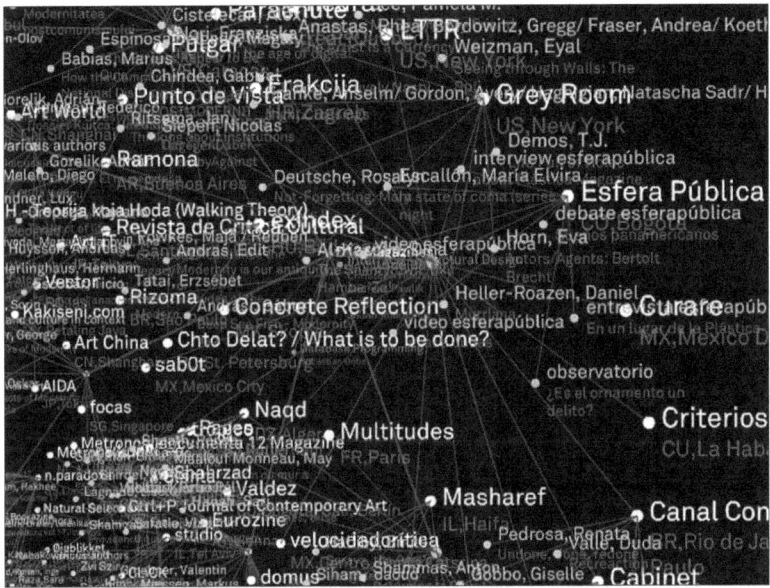

picture 6: Documenta 12 Magazines map

network of micro-events was put forward that would be organised over six months in several venues, communities from peripheral neighbourhoods and the public space. It had significant support from state institutions and local private companies, although there was some initial scepticism.

But the issue is not only that of the reproduction of the exhibition and operation tactics of independent artistic practices but also of the so-called institutional criticism and the critical dynamics of independent publishing projects: in her article *Ascenso y caída del nuevo institucionalismo*, the critic and curator Nina Montmann points out that, what the *"Rooseum and other progressive art institutions had in common was the fact of being institutions of critique, which means institutions that have internalised the institutional criticism formulated by artists of the seventies and nineties, as these institutions had developed self-critique promoted in the first place by the cura-*

The Mag.net Reader 3

tors themselves, who no longer just invited artists who practised criticism but who transformed, primarily on their own initiative, the institutional structures, their hierarchies and functions. The 'institutions of critique', from the mid-nineties onwards, reacted through the criticism of the globalised corporative institutionalism and its production of consumer publics."

One of these reactions is the emphasis made in relation to the public[18]. And an attentive public, for whom consumption is precisely the place of production of a process of self-education. It is no longer a public that has to be trained or fed contents with explanatory texts next to each work. The proposal is thus to conceive the exhibition as a space of dialogue, as the *constitution of a public sphere*[19], as a vehicle of mediation of critical thought, thanks to the articulation of an *organised network*[20] of independent critical publications.

In picture 6 we see the map with names of the publications that make up Documenta 12 Magazines. They are shown connected to each other by some lines, as a representation of possible relations.

What kinds of relations could be suggested between these publications? As Fran Ilich asked some time ago in an interview published in [esfera-pública], are we interested in communicating with each other? If so, how can we foster these spaces of dialogue?

One possibility is to establish temporal links[21] based on issues that can be of common interest for the spaces involved. This would enable the issues to be seen from diverse contexts and perspectives, open the space to other interlocutors, and introduce dynamics that stimulate critical reflection and possibilities of action.

If we consider the possibility of a micro public sphere that goes beyond local borders, it is due both to the effort of the interested publishing projects and the pertinence of the discourses with specific audiences in different parts of the world.

Is there any relationship, for instance, between the ways the crisis of an art institution in Lima is confronted and the way the members of the art world react when faced with the crisis of a similar institution in Bogotá? What can we learn from these situations? What reflections could we exchange with artists from Bilbao and San Sebastián on how the market and globalisation affect the public spheres of art?

In this sense, a discussion in Bogotá could have resonance in Amsterdam, Lima and San Sebastián[22]. But the meaning and continuity of these links will depend more on the processes of self-organisation of different spaces and publics rather than on thinking that a series of issues proposed from a publishing project can be relevant for a *general public* that, as an abstract entity, is in direct relation with the conception of a modern public sphere that only listens to a series of authorised voices.

As a result of the consensual logic of corporate institutionalism, the public is an indicator for measuring impacts and allocated budgets. For artistic practices and the spaces located outside corporate culture the public is a transforming element, to the extent that it is a generator of opinion, disaccord and critical thought.

If there have been changes in the state of things in the artistic world, one of them is precisely the transformation of the *spheres of the public*, as well as the importance that it has now acquired when considering the reception of artistic practices and, in consequence, the structure and functions of the cultural institutions.

Notes

[1] Ribalta, Jorge. Contrapúblicos. http://republicart.net

[2] Habermas, Jürgen. The Structural Transformation of the Public Sphere: An Inquiry into a Category of Bourgeois Society. MIT Press, Cambridge, MA; Polity Press, Cambridge, Great Britain, 1989.

[3] Sheikh, Simon. Public Spheres and the Functions of Progressive Art Institutions. http://republicart.net 2004.

[4] Laddaga points out other authors who have detected such a dynamic and mentions, among others, "Un art contextuel" by Paul Ardenne, "Secrecy and publicity. Reactivating the avantgarde" by Sven Lutticken, the "Estética relacional" by Bourriaud and the critical review of Bourriaud's ideas by Claire Bishop in the journal October in her article "Antagonism and relational aesthetics". Laddaga, Reinaldo. Estética de la emergencia, Adriana Hidalgo editora, 2006.

[5] The members of El Bodegón are the artists Víctor Albarracín, Natalia Ávila, Lorena Espitia, Humberto Junca, Juan Peláez, Edwin Sánchez and Cindy Triana.

[6] According to the introductory text in the Internet portal http://www.lebodegon.org/

[7] Until only a few years ago, the state cultural institutions started a process of democratisation of resources, which at first were aimed at attending to the historical claims of some museums and cultural centres. However, as these are very recent processes – the Secretariat for Culture, Leisure and Sport in Bogotá is in the midst of a restructuring process – apart from the awards and grants programme, it is not clear how to access aid for those projects by artists that involve the production and maintenance of exhibition and publishing projects.

[8] In 1995 the first issue of the journal Tándem was published, featuring a series of meetings that, with the name of "conversations", invited artists to talk about their works – without the intermediary of critics – to a public composed of art students, artists, teachers and other people from the art world.

[9] An independent journal that, according to its editors (François Bucher, Lucas Ospina and Bernardo Ortiz), began as a local dialogue between friends in Colombia and has been careful not to lose the anachronistic meaning it limited itself to – in some way similar to the Pennsylvania Amish which analyses the social effects of each technological thing.

[10] With this editorial project, the artist participated in the Venice Biennale in Bogotá.

[11] Erguida begins to circulate as a systematic pillaging of the rights of an author chosen to constitute an informative platform, which dedicates each issue to an article proposed by

its editor (Guillermo Vanegas). It starts with "ABC del arte contemporáneo" by Hal Foster.

[12]Published by the artist Fernando Uhía.

[13]These are projects that work without any kind of institutional patronage or aid. They reach their public through lists of emails to artists, curators, teachers, students, researchers, officers of cultural institutions, journalists, some collectors and people interested in contemporary artistic practices.

[14]It has been published since 2000 and suspended since 2005.

[15]Founded in 1995 under the name of Red Alterna, it was later called Momento Crítico and changed its name to Esfera Pública in 2000.

[16]Definition given by the curator Jonas Ekeberg to these kinds of progressive institutions in the article "New Institutionalism", in Versted, no. 1, Office for Contemporary Art, Oslo, 2003.

[17] Closed since April 2006 because of financial problems.

[18] This relational emphasis with the public was also reflected in events such as the last – and truncated – version of the Manifesta and, at a local level, in the Encuentro de Medellín 07, proposed – through workshops, conversations in the Casa del Encuentro – as a space of hospitality, which is defined as the temporal disposition of a space, whether physical, discursive or political, in order to welcome others and enable them to set out their interests and positions. Not only were artists invited, but independent publishing spaces and projects also participated.

[19] Bildung, the German term for education, also means "generation" or "constitution" in the sense of generating or constituting a public sphere.

[20] In the sense in which Nina Montmann defines these institutions of criticism: "This conceivable critical institution could for example adopt the form of an 'organised network' operating at international level, strengthening diverse independent and smaller institutions and activities (whether they are alternative, directed by artists or based on research), also establishing temporary platforms in the heart of major institutions."

[21] In the case of [esferapública], links have been created with other spaces through the publication of texts that have some pertinence with the discussion in hand. On other occasions, this relation was through interviews and the publication of discussions around issues such as artistic education, curatorship and criticism.

[22] There are plans to exchange – in the short and medium term – reflections with spaces (Zehar, Arte-nuevo, Arte y crítica, Magazine in situ), which have dealt with themes similar to those approached in [esferapública].

What May We Expect from a Contemporary Channel?

An exchange of ideas between Patricia Canetti and Leandro de Paula

Visibility has become such an essential value for understanding public space in the last century that the media have on the whole assumed a political role with inevitable social ramifications. The origin of this trend is to be located in the prestige attained by mass-media broadcasting in constructing a collective imaginary capable of transforming the sector into a territory for convergence between endless public attention on the one hand, and a handful of private powers on the other.

Television, radio and cinema – Hollywood in particular – were so hugely successful as news and entertainment media in the first half of the 20th century that they became true emblems of their period and consolidated a particular form of communication: the one-to-many model. The rise of powerful international media conglomerates is a more recent sign of this historical process, and has coincided with a new period in which the 'global village' concept is relativising cultural boundaries, and the notion of the nation-state's political sovereignty.

Globalised markets, and the means of producing and stimulating consumption are the backdrop against which we have been continually compelled to review media and cultural practices. It would be no exaggeration to state that advances in telecommunications in the last twenty years have posed a new economy of symbolic exchanges. Néstor Canclini argues that this is the emergence of *transterritorialities*.

This overlap of space and time has become possible due to the growing social uses of the Internet, especially in the last decade. If we view the emergence of virtualized space in terms of the evolution of 20th Century media, we see that the principles of mass media communication are being challenged. . The flow of information is not per se channelled centrally, but all receptors also function as transmitters, immersed in a network for which the notion of exchange poses the best metaphor and *raison d'être*.

Canal Contemporâneo [http://www.canalcontemporaneo.art.br] is sustained by the involvement of Brazil's contemporary art scene, and it acts on and from this basis. In recent years, it has become the main vehicle of communication and a political platform for this scene in Brazil. In practice, its key objective is to lend visibility to the art system in order to criticise and transform it. Difficulties and contradictions in its performance have arisen by taking this particular course. Since its founding in 2001, Canal has increasingly involved artists, curators, critics, researchers, professors, museologists, gallery owners and institutions throughout Brazil. *Canal* addresses the absence of broadly circulated print publications for the visual and technological arts in Brazil. It has struggled against the uninformed lack of interest in art shown by Brazil's mainstream press, which, if they focus on the subject at all, do so only to stoke controversy

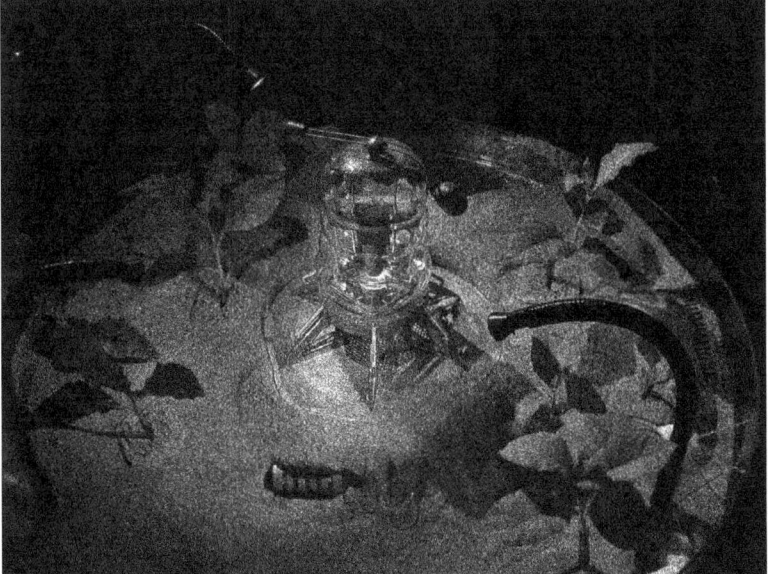

Eduardo Kac, The Eighth Day

around contemporary works, mostly with reactionary arguments. Nevertheless, this existence that occupies a 'gap' might turn Canal into "the voice" of our art scene. And, for this reason, we must be careful of not becoming a mere mirror of a system in which many characteristics of Brazil's socioeconomic inequality are ingrained: an employment market in continuous dialogue with the complexity of commercial and institutional interests.

As a hybrid combining "publishing network" and "digital community", *Canal* is built on the involvement of its own public, which constructs itself as a *vehicle-locus*. There is a real challenge involved in bringing people together to build a community while remaining critical at the same time. This is a continuous balancing act between strengthening ourselves in order to confront external dialogue, and working to transform our own context.

This very brief outline has sought to shed light on the watershed that these new platforms of communication represent for the social history of media. It also suggests certain premises for understanding the impact of this transformation in a situation that has always been relegated to the edges of 'the village' we live in.

In the case of Brazil, the influence of the media – television in particular – has always been associated with the logic of privatisation of public space; a phenomenon with extensive repercussions testing the concept of citizenship, and making consumer behaviour the absolute regulator of collective agendas. Flawed government policies, or the absence of policies, fail to offer social movements representation in the more traditional media. Therefore public attention has gradually shifted away from a more inclusive social interest towards a focus guided by slots on television schedules.

In a country of continental dimensions, with its social structure plagued by severe inequality, this mechanism poses an obvious impasse. Rather than a concern for business marketing strategies, media visibility has become an imperative for existence in and of itself. Only that which is visible actually exists – and thus deserves attention.

Outside this field, an immense space constitutes the 'non-visible edge'. The absence of mechanisms providing visibility has become a cause for concern for authors such as Zygmunt Bauman. In his work, *In Search of Politics*[1], he suggests that the notion of publicising anything that may stir curiosity has become core to the idea of something 'being of public interest'. The 'public' has been stripped of its differential content and left with no agenda of its own. Richard Sennett's *The Fall of Public Man*[2] also looks at the way this 'hollowing-out' prioritises the private sphere and erodes collective beliefs and ideals.

I have sketched an extensive scenario pointing to the core concerns of the contemporary neo-liberal project. Certainly the discussion is much broader than that which has been posed here, but it leads directly to the obstacles we face when we attempt to consolidate digital communities while aiming to transform their socio-political context.

We have witnessed some signs of political transformation in recent years in *Canal Contemporâneo*, but not without making great efforts to break down the political inertia and apathy present in Brazilian visual arts. Given the legacy of the recent military dictatorship, the lack of communication in the arts, the dearth of specialised publications and the recent economic recession, financial survival has been our priority. Within this context, it was almost impossible to imagine how this community would respond to a call for political positioning.

Meant originally as a channel that funnels information on artistic events, *Canal* is now also flexing its muscle in terms of criticising art and cultural policies, targeting the mainstream press, major institutions, and government bodies at different times. In the beginning, the act of publishing a text attacking an agency of public power prompted silence among the online community, but much discussion offline. For example, our first online petition succeeded in halting plans for a Guggenheim Museum in Rio de Janeiro, yet it caused a rift in the community, and a long silence followed.

With broader access, use of the Internet has often assumed a celebratory democratic air, wherein consumers of information supposedly become actual producers. We are dealing with technologies that promise redemption in many ways, such as overcoming the limitations of geo-referenced space and enjoying instantaneous multilateral communication. These aspects of cyberspace could potentially have an enormous societal impact. However, the dynamics governing the use of this new environment may be disguising new problems.

Rather than new problems, perhaps what we are seeing are merely new arrangements of old issues, combined with new technologies. The responsibility for publishing or publicising – the decision to speak out or remain silent – is now being shared by many, but this does not necessarily generate a collective awareness of the process and its importance. Nor does it instigate commitment to maintain what people are creating collectively, or insight into the growing demands made by technology. As an everyday vehicle for news and discussion, *Canal* serves as a collective memory of Brazilian contemporary art, and its production in the broadest sense. But to whom does all this matter?

The internet appears to have fallen prey to its own speed and banality. We use it without noticing differences, and eventually experience new media as "more of the same", although in practice there is something quite different... Seven years ago, *Canal Contemporâneo* saw generating critical reflection on the contemporary art scene as its major challenge. Now it sees itself as subjected to more wide-ranging standards set by the major media. Its own growth represents an impasse: how to widen our collective horizons without being taken over by market interests, as many digital communities did? The question is this: how can we build a living space, not just as an organism enlivened by a group of people, but one configured to allow constant reinvention in relation to existing attitudes, including those related to the actual technological media we are working in?

On launching the tactical media study *Como atiçar a brasa* (How to stoke the fire) as a blog 'inciting' discussions with the press, I drew a parallel between *Canal* and Eduardo Kac's biobot,[3] I whose activity also depends on the multiplication and movement of living beings. However, unlike the micro-organisms giving life to the biobot, the behavioural patterns directing *Canal* are comprised of a complex of individuals and collectives. It is this dynamic that generates our content, and at the same time provides the focus we want to subvert. It takes us back to the notion of reflection as visibility on *Canal*... Finally, what can we expect from a contemporary channel?

The autonomy conferred on new media in terms of broadcasting values and opinions has given many individuals a historically privileged opportunity to spread their own ideas. One of the main obstacles for *Canal Contemporâneo* in consolidating its hybrid proposal – being simultaneously a digital publication and a digital community – is precisely orchestrating these individualities and *transterritorialities* as different spatial-temporal relationships, in the ambit of Brazilian contemporary art.

Initiating dialogue for this collective of professionals and organisations is itself a strategy for representing it. In this respect, this media has the arduous everyday task of being the arena for a debate that did not previously exist. And one that is becoming increasingly more sensitive, as this channel develops to host new positions, contributions and needs.

A channel that strives to be contemporary must be a narrative open to different appropriations, without surrendering to the risks of indefinition. New technologies suggest we are living in a period in which spaces for visibility no longer have to be dominated by a 'handful of private powers'. However, if we are to realise this idea, we must encourage new conceptions of power to emerge and revive the meaning of 'public' by reconciling individual and collective interests within media experience. In other words, we see 'publishing the public' as an absolutely contemporary means of developing *micropolitics*.

Notes

[1] BAUMAN, Zygmunt. *In Search of Politics*. Cambridge: Polity Press, 1999.

[2] SENNETT, Richard. *The fall of public man*. Cambridge: Cambridge University Press, 1974.

[3] Eduardo Kac, The Eighth Day, 2001 (detail). Transgenic artwork with biological robot (biobot), GFP plants, GFP amoebae, GFP fish, GFP mice, audio, video, Internet. http://www.ekac.org/8thday.html

Publishing the Public: Why bother?

Jelena Vesic

Publishing is often understood as the process of production and dissemination of literature or information, and as the activity whose purpose
is making information available for public view. But, publishing also mobi-
lises the complex relationships between content and exchange, statement and practice, intentions and effects, the start and end points in the
global circulation of material and immaterial goods.

Therefore, I would like to share some impressions about the organisation of work and material-social effects of the so-called 'production of
content' through the 'gesture of publishing'. What is the role of content,
and how does it function in the broader social and economical sphere?
What are the material conditions of circulation of printed matter? What
is the 'destiny' of content production within the economically regulated
field of culture? In other words, how does this 'content', produced by
individual or collective subjects, operate within the hegemonous logic of
communication and exchange of the international art scene?

The international art scene is definitely not an institution in the narrow
sense of the word: its main characteristic is heterogeneity of all kinds.
But, the symbolic activity of production and dissemination of aesthetic
objects and ideas, which is at work here, clearly reproduces the economical structures of global society with all the heterogeneity, mobility and
flexibility embedded in the latter. The formal presence and functioning of
the international scene is regulated through grandiose artistic, media,
music and performance manifestations, conceived to demarcate safe ter-
ritories of representation of 'global(ised) friendship'. Being part of this
scene requires continuous self-education, self-promotion and networking, that is, the entrepreneurial-managerial activities of the independent
intellectuals who are self-employed, and who are obliged to produce
content as their proper work, but at the same time are forced to 'crea-
tively organise' their working environment.

All this points to the dual processes of culturalisation of the economy
and the economisation of culture, which is the characteristic for contemporary neo-liberal capitalist conditions. Today, 'Intellectual production', or the 'need to know', or 'the love for beauty', are becoming the

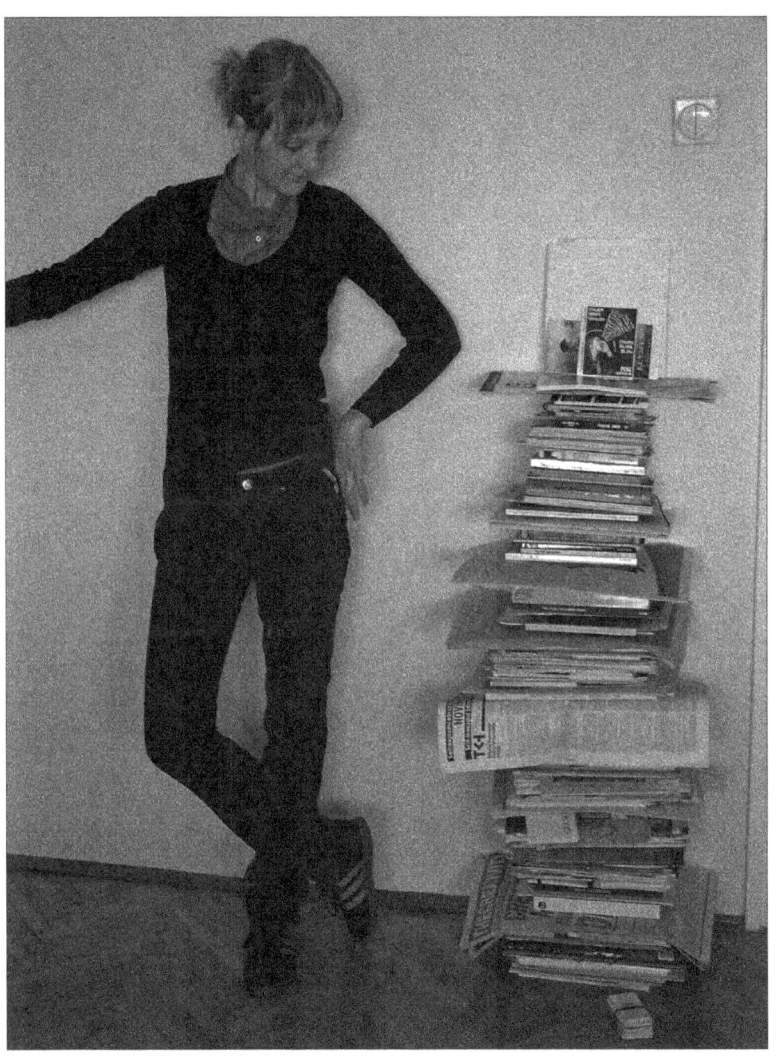

main outlets open to economic development. Discussing the concept of 'immaterial labour', Maurizio Lazzarato underlines the new subjective-political composition of the working class, and the informational-cultural content of the commodity.[1] Besides participating in the production of cultural content, the so-called 'creative workers', 'content producers' or 'content providers' are involved in "defining and fixing cultural and artistic standards, fashion, taste, consumer norms, and, more strategically, public opinion". According to Lazzarato, immaterial labour constitutes itself in forms that are immediately collective, and that exist only in the form of networks and flows. The organisation of the cycle of production is not obviously apparent to the eye, because it is not defined by the four walls of the factory, but rather operates in society at large, at the territorial level that he calls the "basin of immaterial labour". This definition of the territorial level – of the 'factory without the walls' – fits very much in the institutional *modus operandi* of the international art scene. Instead of being subjected to the production on a simple command, workers are today 'the active subjects'. The role of contemporary 'content producers' is to promote continual innovation in the forms and conditions of communication. The new 'creative industries' teach us that "we should all become subjects", which sounds like an unambiguous requirement for the subjectivities that are rich in knowledge, that is, involved in management, decision-making and handling the information.

I made an *ad hoc*-artwork, or – to be fully precise – one household installation, spontaneously created as an emergency solution for the lack of storage space, since all the bookshelves have been overloaded for quite some time. This artificial storage technique spontaneously, or less spontaneously, depicts the processes of accumulation of content, circulation of information, and the creation of networks, as the syndromes of contemporary cultural production. A short statement in the conceptualist style may sound like:

"This is a tower of printed matter, a piece of 'administrative aesthetics', which shows material evidence of my working and networking at the international art scene during the year 2007."

It is built of different books, catalogues, magazines, journals, newspapers, brochures and leaflets; semi-read, quickly-read or not-read-at-all. Its singular-contents came to be thought over mostly through postponing – like 'one day I will read all this'. It is, in a way, an ethnographic piece about the art world, which provides information about one year of curatorial travels, and the average amount of 'objects of communication' that one member of the art community gathers while encountering other people during various exhibitions, conferences, residency programmes, etc. The conceptual gesture of accumulation of books produces a tautological overlap of the objects and subjects of communication. It creates a literary reified, non-usable archive of all the content [re]produced through the communication and exchange with different cultural actors over a one-year period of time. I mentioned the term 'aesthetics of administration', proposed by Benjamin Buchloh and its connection to the questioning of art institutions and their bureaucratic apparatuses, since it is closely related to works with paper, documents and publishing.

This little archive does not represent any subjective memory of its owner, nor is there a hierarchy conditioned in any way by the logic of the attention economy. It is rather a 'neutral' volume of printed matter, assembled according to a certain principle. This communication piece also cannot be taken as the analogue representation of networks, because networks do not imply a one and singular sink-channel, but are administrated through numerous nodes, [repeating the mechanism of participatory management on a smaller scale]. For Geert Lovink, the process of networking is fine *"as far as it integrates the plurality of forces [...] as well as the persistence of dispute or disagreement [...] But the primary questions remain: where does it go? how long does it last?[...] but also: who is speaking? and: why bother?"* [...] *"Networks will never be rewarded and 'embedded' in well-functioned structures. Just as the modernist avant-garde saw itself punctuating the fringes of society, so to have tactical media taken comfort in the idea of targeted micro-interventions"*.[2] This is, of course, not the case with all the networks, especially with those that stem from the logic of 'free cooperation', and are conducted by the current interests of various cultural subjects. The tower of prints as the personal embodiment of the process of networking poses the question about the "outside" of networks, that is, about the economic models behind all this performance of communication.

In the classic art historical framework, the content of this "sculpture" reflects the position of speech, as established in the modernist environment by Gustave Courbet and his painting *The Painter's Studio: A Real Allegory*, and quite often quoted in conceptual art theory as the model for questioning the art institution. But, while in the case of Courbet this position is framed by an atelier and artistic figure of lonesome genius, here it is ultimately public, social and even impossible without the elements of 'public socialising'. The modernist institution of culture, examined and criticised by Courbet as well as the conceptualists, and represented through the national museum or private market-oriented gallery, is replaced nowadays by the different organisation of intellectual labour, change of economical discourse, and by the less formal structure of the global art scene.

Therefore, my household installation, archival experiment, or conceptual joke, points to the feverish networking of people and ideas as the basic function of the 'gesture of publishing', no matter what its original intentions and particular aims are. How much of this volume of heavy material can be consumed as 'content'? How much of it can be carefully read and critically observed? Or does it only serve as a sign of good relations between the donor and the receiver, in order to maintain the 'language of politeness' in the contemporary art world? Here, we can also ask what actually constitutes the content, because the content is framed, not only by the written texts and critical thought, but also by its circulation and institutionalisation.

We can claim that there is definitely something like 'the language of politeness', which establishes itself as the inevitable tool for communication in contemporary art. The literacy of cultural politeness implies a *savoir-faire* about how to summarise your current projects, how to express your interest when hearing about the undertakings of your interlocutors, and how to be prepared for the exchange of business cards, leaflets and publications with other colleagues from the art scene. This institutionalised language actually serves to administrate the process of global networking in the field of culture: it reproduces a state of a friendship within 'the institution of art', and offers a form to communicate and negotiate with all the members of the art community. It is normative and hierarchical, but open for improvisation and demonstration of individual virtuosity. I would compare it to the court communication of the 16th-18th centuries, and the birth of the social role of 'educated gentlemen'. Today, this role is succeeded by the role of members of the international art community. On the one hand, it requires a so-called openness, and politeness towards artists, cultural workers, art institutions and sponsors. It implies unquestionable support for the current production, whatever it is and however it is organised. It maintains a *status quo* of the existing order. On the other hand, it appears to be the consequence of compelling requests for a 'collective debate', 'exchange of opinions' and 'creation of networks'. This is typical for all the cultural environments aspiring towards critical thinking, and re-examination of the existing state of affairs, but also within this specific circumstances they are forced to overproduce, and therefore compelled to join to the all-pervasive 'market of ideas'.

Contemporary neo-liberal capitalism demands the worker's personality and subjectivity to be involved in the production of value, which means the independent cultural worker is responsible not only for his/her own

The Mag.net Reader

enthusiasm and motivation, but also for his/her own self-presentation as a unique 'cultural personae'. Continual innovation is one of the imperatives of this demand, but the kind of innovation is conceived as an institutional and economic project.

Notes

[1] Maurizio Lazzarato, *Immaterial Labour*,
[http://www.generation-online.org/c/fcimmateriallabour3.htm]

[2] Geert Lovink, *The Principle of Notworking, Concepts in Critical Internet Culture*, HvA Publicaties, Amsterdam, 2005.

Hacktivist Publishing.

"Another Culture is Possible" – not Impossible!

A conversation between Fran Ilich[1] and Cornelia Sollfrank[2],
Celle, 23 July, 2007

Cornelia Sollfrank: Fran, you are on your way from Kassel to Berlin. You took part in the magazine project during the paper and pixel week organized by Alessandro Ludovico and Nat Muller in Kassel. I would like to ask you to share your experiences from that week and also tell me about the work you do in Mexico. What magazine did you represent at the Documenta?

Fran Ilich: The magazine is called sab0t, and it is a printed pamphlet, tabloid size magazine. Every issue has a different topic, and the basic idea of the magazine is to bring the strategies of art and net culture, but also subversive information, to an audience that would normally not connect online. This newspaper is part of possibleworlds.org, which is an autonomous, cooperative server on the Internet.

C.S.: If you were online, why and when did you decide to go for a printed edition of your magazine too?

F.I.: I found out that it is difficult to communicate with many of the people that I would be interested in having a conversation with, simply because they would not go online – for many different reasons. So, I decided to make that effort and go for a paper issue. When it is economically possible, we go and print an issue. We ask for different funders and friends to give around $50 each, or whatever is needed for printing, and then ask the people to give whatever contribution they want.

C.S.: You said sab0t is a project of the server possibleworlds.org. What exactly is this server for?

F.I.: It provides hosting space to 40 different projects, mainly in Mexico, but some of them are also in Germany, Peru, Brazil, Barcelona, or in Costa Rica. The idea is to create a kind of a virtual community space, a common ground that is nourishing to us in many ways.

C.S.: But only printed magazines were invited to the Documenta

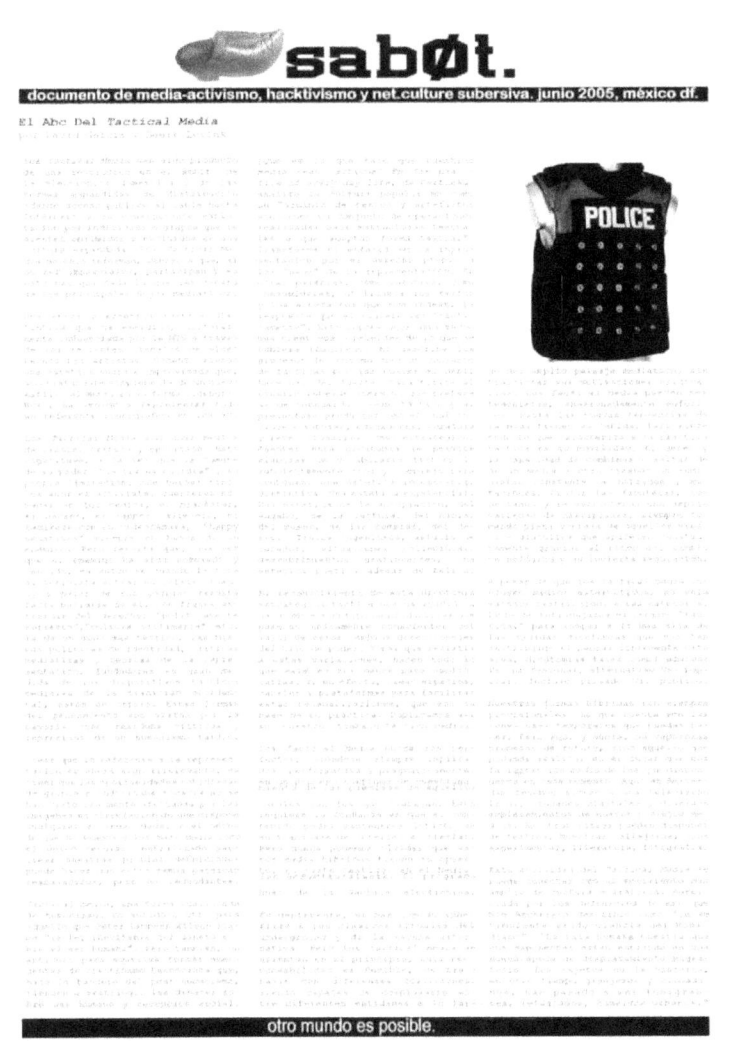

Magazine project, right?

F.I.: Well, mostly, but a few are also only online, e.g. Esfera Publica from Bogotá in Colombia. They used to have printed magazines in previous years, but no longer do. But as they have about 3,000 subscribers for their mailing list, for example, and their web services, they cannot be ignored. They are doing a lot of important work about the public sphere in Colombia.

C.S.: The background of my question is that I was wondering what role digital media and the Internet play for the Documenta curators. Do they recognize the potential of the Internet as a medium to organize people, to build "small media" and to develop new activist and artistic strategies, and also new aesthetic experiences? Or does the "world's biggest show of contemporary art" – as they describe it themselves – still focus on pre-digital communication and media. What is your impression about the relation between the printed and the online part of the magazine project?

F.I.: My impression is that so far I still don't own the copies of the printed magazines, mainly because I didn't want to carry all the weight from Kassel to Celle, to Berlin to Madrid, to Philadelphia to San Diego, and back to Tijuana... even if they were in my backpack on the airplane. The fact is that everything has been published online and I can read every text that was chosen to be printed, plus all the others that were much less mainstream and more interesting for my own practice. So I wouldn't want to carry the weight of so many texts I'm less interested in and that don't communicate very much to me. I prefer the b-side much more, even in records. The same thing happened with the exhibition. I was more interested in more off-beat material. Fortunately the network is vast and infinite, and we can have all wonderful connections going through different sides. Like the Tijuana of today, which doesn't depend much on Downtown and posher parts. The city is becoming hyper-communicated through different streets and roads in ways that some years ago wouldn't make any sense at all. Now it is not a necessity for all parts of the city to connect to the main roads. In the same way, I learned about the existence of Documenta because of Documenta X. Specifically through works such as Kein Mensch ist Illegal, Bordercamp, or the very First Cyberfeminist International, which were all part of the Hybrid Work Space by Eike Becker and Geert Lovink/Pit Schultz. I believe back then these were not too central to the Documenta itself. Anyhow, eventually the book of the Documenta Magazines project will arrive at my postal address, and by then the online discussion will be somewhere else, and the book will go to the shelves.

C.S.: Do you have any idea what the criteria were for selecting the projects? As many as possible? From as many different countries as possible?

F.I.: I can only guess about it. The guy behind the Magazine project, Georg Schöllhammer, is very much aware of both the printed, as well as the digital world. But as Documenta is a contemporary art thing, this is perhaps why it was more focused on print.

C.S.: Excuse me, I don't understand this explanation. Why is art automatically more related to print?

F.I.: Of course, it's not, but this is how institutions traditionally think.

C.S.: Has there been any discussion about it?

F.I.: In the beginning, yes. And they were also looking for mailing lists. But where we ended up, the "paper & pixel" section, is this kind of hybrid space: publications working with digital culture on and offline, and contemporary art publications working online. And sab0t is more of a zine, very cheaply produced, in contrast to most of the other more glossy magazines. It can be distributed online as a .pdf, or printed as a cheap black and white publication.

C.S.: Now, let's talk about the event in Kassel. What did you do there, and what were your experiences?

F.I.: For me, it was part of a long process, because I actually met Georg in 2002 in Seville at Post-Media Publishing, which was an event organized by Andreas Broeckmann at the Universidad Internacional de Andalucía. It was about digital magazines that had decided to also produce printed issues. As I have been involved in a number of projects (e.g. Sputnik, Undo, Cinematik and others), I was invited there. The idea back then was to create a kind of platform to exchange texts between these different magazines that were mainly Western and Eastern European. But it turned out to be very difficult to exchange texts, because of language reasons, because of economical reasons, but mainly because of the different contexts. I think Georg's project is addressing this fact and trying to introduce traditional art magazines more than digital magazines into this dialogue. For example, there has been an introduction to alternative licensing models, like copyleft.

C.S.: Where did that happen?

F.I.: At the platform Editors.documenta.de[4]. So, basically, we were invited to exchange texts with each other, imagining, for instance, to have a

Mexican text in a Chinese magazine. I don't know how much of this has become a success.

C.S.: And what was your concrete experience?

F.I.: Sab0t has been invited by the Brazilian magazine canal contemporaneo to exchange texts, and also by Ramona – an Argentinean magazine. But this may vary from magazine to magazine, of course. Maybe we have weird texts that do not make any sense for other contexts, like mainstream magazines?

C.S.: What else was going on – besides the possibility of finding exchange partners for cross-publishing?

F.I.: There were a couple of panels and internal workshops on topics like "the art of blogging" etc. And there were fierce discussions between those who are in favor of blogging and others who are against it. There were also other discussions, about translation, which is always an important issue. And of course, the most interesting things are those discussions off the record, the conspiracies, the informal exchange between the magazines that are already collaborating on a more effective level. And, of course, for the people who were invited to Kassel, it was a chance to see the exhibition.

C.S.: Are you happy that you came the long way from Mexico? What are you taking back? What does it mean to you that you participated?

F.I.: I was really happy to be here, to have the chance to have a dialogue with the Documenta, because this means being able to escape the usual state structures in Mexico. And, among other things, I had the opportunity to talk to José Carlos Mariátegui, a Peruvian researcher, who has some relation to Casa José Carlos Mariátegui (his grandfather was a seminal 20th century Latin American revolutionary who still turns heads around). We discussed the possibility of him inviting me for a residency, so that I could do research and write about Zapatista internet practices, which is something that has been surrounded in mythology. Then I had a good exchange with the Colombians. Also to see this Documenta thing and try to understand why it is so big. I saw a couple of pieces that made me think a lot: an Argentinean piece called Tucumán Arde about some artists from the 1960s and 1970s who were trying to show the situation in a remote, rural region of their country that had a major crisis, and how they were fighting the institutions then, 30 years ago. And I also enjoyed

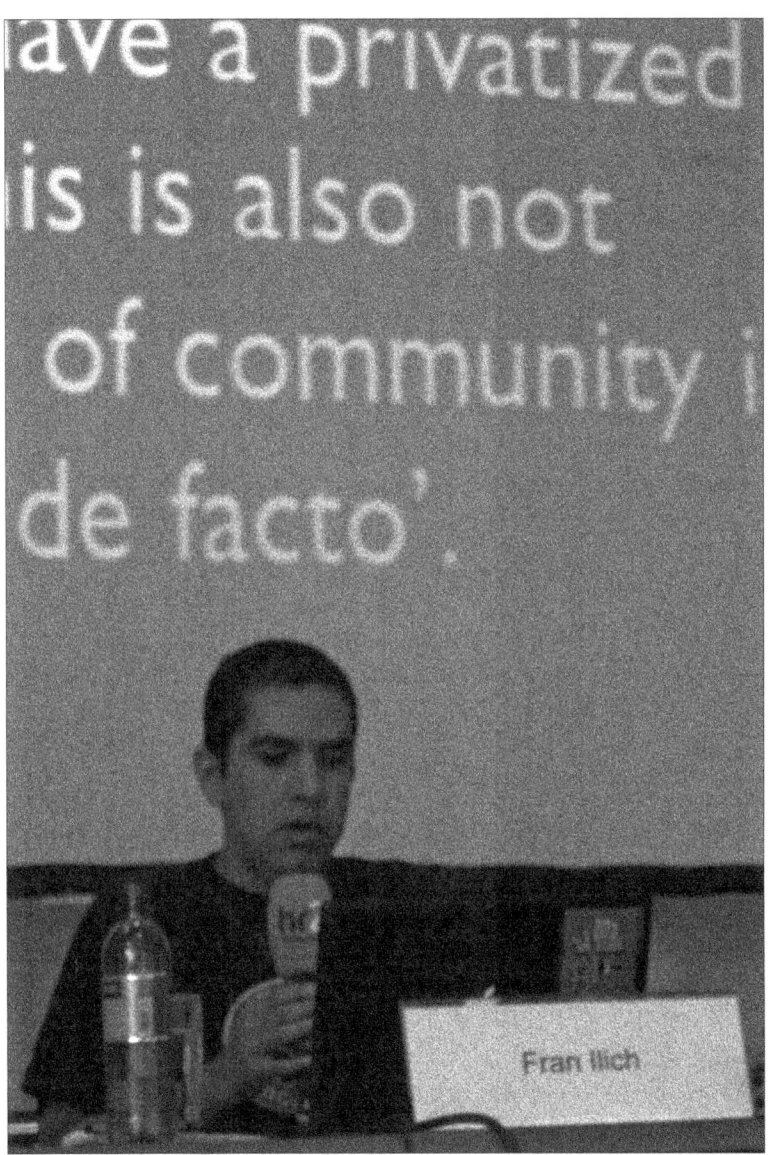

Fran Ilich at Documenta 12

a Brazilian piece a lot, I forgot the name of the author but it was some people interviewing more people on the streets, and of course, "9 Scripts from a Nation at War" in the Documenta Halle about the Afghanistan processes in the US.

C.S.: What does it mean for your local work that you have been here. Will anything be different when you get back?
F.I.: No, I guess it will be the same. I mean, at a certain point, when I first received the invitation from Documenta, I talked to the director of a state institution, who then agreed to fund three issues of our sab0t magazine (we are talking about $1,200 here). But when they started to notice that we were not willing to publish their press releases and other stuff they'd suggested, they decided to not give us the money.

C.S.: What kind of institution was it? A museum?
F.I.: It was a very important digital art institution. For me this was helpful to get to know better the state of the current situation. It is very difficult to have a dialogue with institutions in Mexico.

C.S.: How did you experience your role in Kassel, the role you played within Documenta? Do you have the impression that your work is taken seriously there? Did you get serious support? Were you treated well?
F.I.: Well, during this week, I was taken as seriously as any other editor who was there. The magazine projects had a space where the magazines were glued (!) on the table, about a hundred magazines ... people could browse them, and get to know what was going on in other countries. It was definitely too much information for a passer-by, but it was great to be there. But the Documenta boss did not show up, neither did his wife. Probably, I was an exotic guest inside Documenta, but I don't have anything against being exotic, even in Mexico City I am exotic: being from Tijuana. I speak with a different accent than the people in Mexico City. For me it is less offensive to be exotic than to be a person who thinks of a person from another culture as being exotic.

C.S.: What is the role of Documenta for artists and activists, for the people you are working with in Mexico?
F.I.: Most people I am working with or who are working within possible worlds do not know what Documenta is. They say, "Ah, Kassel! But where is Kassel? Sorry for my ignorance. Oh, it's Germany, great, let's do it!" But there are others who know what Documenta is, and it certainly plays a major role in the art world of Mexico. Everybody wants to be

there. For example, there was a piece in front of Orangerie, in which a collective from Mexico, Laboratorio Curatorial 060, collaborated with the work of another artist. We are working with them in Mexico. I am not that important. But many official artists who had expected or hoped to be invited were not here. There is this tendency among people in Mexico to undermine things when they are not included. For example, when ARCO, the Spanish contemporary art fair, decided to invite Mexico as the official guest, hundreds of people traveled to Spain, and I was not one of them. But the newspapers in Spain would quote me as one of the Mexicans. For me that was really offensive, because I am not one of the 700, or 300, or 100 official artists in Mexico. For me it is an offence to be a Mexican in this context. Or, when Mexico was invited to Haus der Kulturen der Welt in 2001 or 2002, I was also not invited. Although the topic was "borders"–something that I have worked on a lot, but from a very critical perspective. So the battle line, or the positions, are very clear. We have the same passports. But that's it. I have never received any grants or any support from the Mexican embassy to travel or anything.

C.S.: Before, you said one sentence that seems to be very central for me. You said that the idea of your magazine is to bring art and culture to the movement and not the other way round, to bring political activism into the art spaces. Do you have any explicit experiences with bringing activism to the art world?

F.I.: I don't think that it is necessarily wrong to do so, but it is very difficult to establish a common ground. For example, people in the institutions would tell me to bring my Zapatista mask to talks, wear it, for example... I mean, they need to show they are inclusive, which of course they are not.

C.S.: Ricardo Dominguez did that for many years, wearing the Zapatista mask at art events.

F.I.: Yes, but he did in the US. Here, I mean, in Mexico, I can't do it, because the Zapatistas gave up their dialogue with the government in 1994, because the government did not keep the promises they had made before. So, I can't simply wear the mask in the art context. That would mean to mix things that should better be separated. This year, for example, we were invited to participate in the second edition of the same festival. First I was invited as a candidate for the post of director. Then they said I would not have the necessary credentials to do the job. Then, they invited me as a curator, which was fantastic because the topic was "borders and communities". But when they found out what I wanted to do, they told me they did not want to get involved in politics, but rather politics in more poetic ways. And finally they invited me as an artist, but they still refused adequate payment. So we are still in the middle of negotiations. We at least want to keep the hardware we used in the exhibition, because otherwise we would be totally exploited there. It's there that we are exotic, and we would be used as part of their justification mechanisms in order to demonstrate democracy to the outside world. We know we are getting used there, but OK, it does not matter as long as we get certain things there, e.g. a satellite modem, digital projectors, computers.

C.S.: You want to make a deal with them?
F.I.: Yes, we are asking to establish a kind of a work-station in a closed space with one entrance only. If you want to get in, you have to sign a petition, including your passport number. The petition is a complaint about the classicist art system, about the failure of the dialogue with the Zapatistas, about the presidential election fraud, and it includes the demand for the immediate release of all political prisoners. The petition will be signed by the actual people who come to the exhibition. Probably the director of the place is not going to sign it. Nor ambassadors or important figures. So this is our way of participating in the exhibition. What we are stating is that we are there, in the exhibition, but at the same time, what we are doing can only be seen by the people who sign this petition. And the people who don't sign it will not be able to see what we are doing–which is good. Amongst other things, we are planning an alternative symposium there with people who do pirate radio, net art etc.

C.S.: Part of the Zapatista's policies is to build "another culture". What does that look like? Because this is also where you come from, right?
F.I.: We are collaborating with other collectives, other than possible-worlds.org, thinking and trying to create an alternative television system, an alternative radio system, using different values from those supported by the Mexican state and corporations. We have been working on tele-novelas, we are going to open a media space in Tijuana in a couple of months, which will be founded by individual members, working on street graphics, indymedia, printing zines, doing documentary work ...And there will be the Fiction Department, a group dedicated to narrative media

research and production. And I guess that's it.

C.S.: So, your main projects are alternative radio and TV projects, as well as public space projects, including the Internet.
F.I.: Exactly, everything to communicate with a non-elitist culture.

C.S.: How is the economy of this work?
F.I.: Precarious. It is an unpaid volunteer-work economy. But this is exactly what we have to do, we have to find a way to make our work sustainable, otherwise, we are going to be sick in five years and die young... What we do is that we only work a couple of hours a day, that is OK.

C.S.: So the idea of "another culture" means being paid and supported by the people, by the community, through a subscription model or micro-payments systems, for example?
F.I.: There are different models being used by different collectives. I decided to go for the cooperative, which means I get part of my income through writing etc. but also do other work. Usually, the ones who can give away their work for free have parents who give them money. What many people do is to move back to smaller towns where life is cheaper, and where it is also easier to get in touch with different social groups, e.g. older generations. I was reading the new book by Alberto Hijar last month, who is somebody I really admire. I would love to get to know him personally, and talk to him about electronic media, because he has been working for 30 years, involved in the whole of Latin-American cinema, and the theater of the oppressed (Augusto Boal); he is very experienced, and he could probably give us good advice. But it is so difficult to bridge the generation gap. Maybe we would seem very naive to him, making all the wrong decisions, yes, maybe that is the case; we should talk about it. And also, I could not afford a university education. I am doing it now, late. I feel like I am doing everything backwards. I don't have money to continue this next semester.

C.S.: What is the heritage of Western culture, of modernity? What does it mean for your work? Is it important?
F.I.: Yes, very much. It took me 19 years to find out that I was Latin-American. Growing up close to the border, I was always exposed to US-American radio and television, and media; at the same time we were

much neglected by the Mexicans, being just a poor town far away from Mexico City. So I was reading French and German literature before I read Latin American literature. Latin America looked so outdated to me. But of course, when I started living in the US, going to raves, meeting cyber-punks, meeting Mexican and Latin writers in the US, I found out that I was completely white trash, Tijuana white trash. And so in a way I finally understood what being Latin American meant. Years later, when I moved back to Mexico, I started to read Latin American literature and got aware of all this. I started Latin American studies as a B.A. I still have not finished it because now I want to know everything. I want to know about the revolutions, and the colonial period, and meet all the people from these countries. And this is where I can communicate with Europeans, for instance, because in a strange, hybrid, bastard way, I am mixing all this together. Of course, when I make a TeleNouvelle-Vague, it is Godard in a Mexican low-aesthetics way. Like the Border Hack[5] was a kind of off-spring of Florian Schneider's Border Camp, then I used to work with a cyberfeminist, Cindy Gabriela Flores, who also is very dedicated to working in Mexico.

C.S.: Do you think that the principles of democracy and the way the art world functions do exclude each other? Is art bound to be elitist? This is a question that not only concerns Mexico, but the whole world. Who has the power to define what art and culture should be? When I look at the Documenta exhibition, I wonder how backward-oriented, and even blind to contemporary aesthetical discourse such an institution can be. And—sorry to say this—it's great that you guys were there, but I am afraid that it is totally on the side and fulfills a more decorative function than anything else. Although I have to admit that the magazine project has huge potential – the role it plays within Documenta, the way it is represented and communicated, is ridiculous.

F.I.: Things are not going on, on the highways, but on the side. Maybe you have to take some bad roads, go to a small town, in order to discover something fantastic. For example, in 2003 I was invited to go to Talent Campus at the Berlinale, the Berlin film festival, and I was excited to meet people who are making cinema in Asia and Africa. But when I got there, what I saw was a representation of the world film industry. There were Mexicans, but from the Mexican institutions, lots from France, lots from the US, lots from the UK and Germany. I felt very disappointed when I saw this. It seems it is all about national representation, while the logics of the Internet are about individuals interacting. This is something I like best about the whole nettime scene; you don't have to pass through the President's office in order to get to Hamburg.

C.S.: The title of your newspaper is sab0t and presumably has something to do with the idea of sabotage, which is a certain way to "react" to something.

F.I.: Oh, yeah, this has been criticized a lot by colleagues with Zapatista affinities. They were asking me why I am still in a dialogue with institutions, why I am staying within the logics of sabotage while it has been proven repeatedly that it does not work. The only thing I can say is, I am Mestizo, I am from the border, I am an artist. My mother was in an artist group in the 1960s and 70s. This group became very big, but she left for a small town to live her life as a teacher. This is not what I want to do. In a way I think it is mediocre. On the other side, it looks like the right and healthy choice, and is probably the more intelligent thing to do. I feel that I am at a very difficult point. The question is: What to do? Or to speak from tradition: What is to be done?

Notes

[1] http://www.thing-hamburg.de/index.php?id=688

[2] http://www.thing-hamburg.de/index.php?id=415

[3] http://www2.unia.es/arteypensamiento04/aesthetics/aesthetics01/frame.html

[4] http://editors.documenta.de

[5] http://www.noborder.org/camps/01/mex/display.php?id=56

Why MoreIsMore / Network Distribution System?

The OpenMute team Feb 2008

services@metamute.org, Licence: none, free2share

http://moreismore.net/

Change in the Signals/Signs of Identity: Modernity Tinged with Post-Modernity. 1982 - 1994

MoreIsMore (working title Network Distribution System, or NDS) is a national and international platform seeking to tackle long-standing problems that cultural organisations suffer with the offline distribution of their products (typically books, magazines, catalogues, sound recordings, films). NDS provides a web portal where producers, couriers, resellers and others involved in the promotion and distribution of such goods can negotiate and administer the entire sales process from order to fulfilment. Using the most up-to-date web based tools and a social networking paradigm, the site functions as a market place and support structure to the cultural sector, improving participants' visibility, efficiency and overall sustainability through trade at national and international level. The title MoreIsMore puns on the modernist dictum 'Less is More' – whose use in the Bauhaus and by Buckminster Fuller was indexed to utility (of technology and form) – to highlight the wealth of material being produced in all corners of this country, and make this available for purchase to all.

The distribution companies upon which the cultural sector has come to rely do not, in our opinion, operate on the kinds of premises which can work towards the creation of a useful, evolving support structure. Their difficult position vis a vis the market place – especially as it functions on the high street – means profit margins have to be strictly observed and more experimental material is sidelined. There are other incompatibilities to consider; small producers for example often have insufficient administrative capacity to cope with a commercial relationship with a distributor. (Processing and fulfilling purchase orders, creating invoices and ensu-

The Mag.net Reader 3

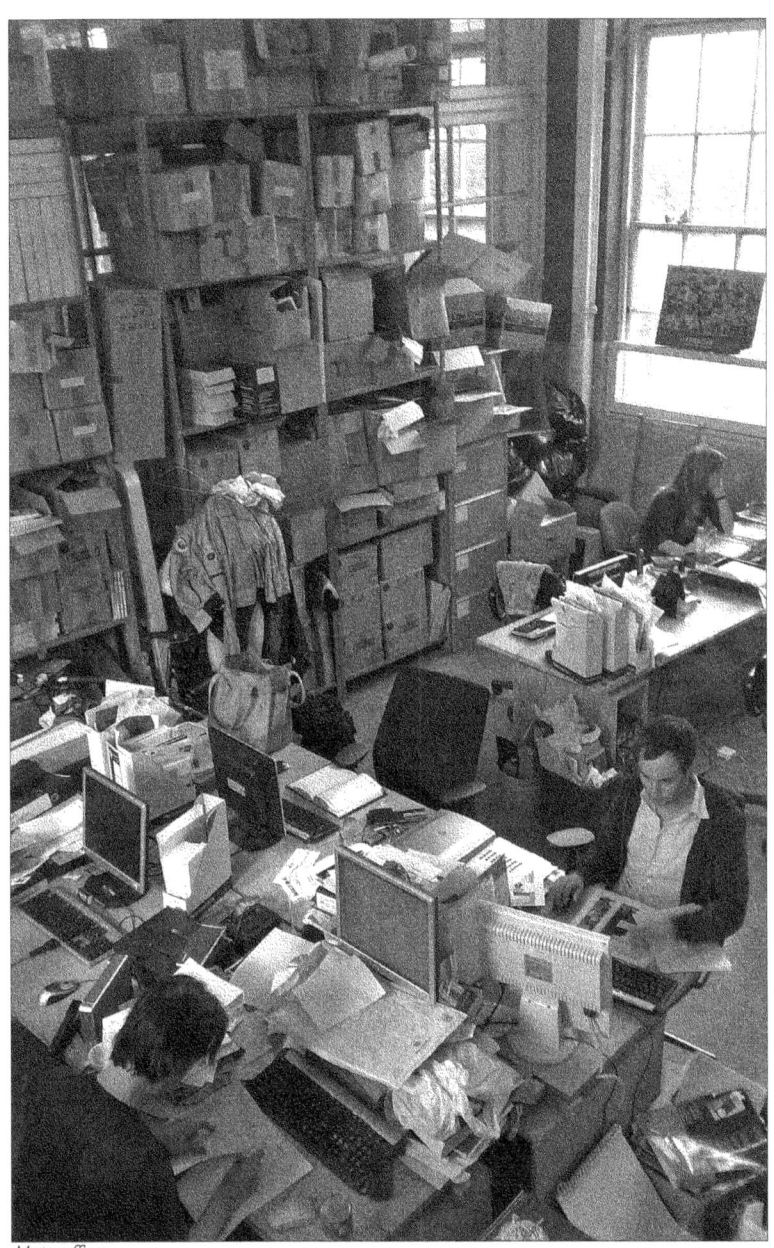

Mute offices

ring they are paid are not a first priority for these cultural outfits and this creates an enormous Achilles heel for them when trying to sell and be remunerated for goods.)

The warehousing model most distributors still use causes organisational inefficiencies and concomitant vulnerabilities vis a vis online retailers such as Amazon, which has moved aggressively into 'non-mainstream' sectors. At the international level, the picture is further complicated by distributors' lack of truly localised knowledge of customer interest, frequently obstructing a match between product and buyer in 'peripheral' locations and causing a general drift towards the homogenisation of supply (the sole availability of big-brand titles). Product-diversity becomes restricted to hot-spot outlets such as the mega-institutions (Tate, Guggenheim, etc.) and dominant chains (Borders), which can afford to use alternative titles to create a 'destination shopping experience', and generally leverage them to create added value for the outlet as a whole. Lastly, distributors arguably also lack the kind of detailed sectoral understanding that could keep their operational models in step with those of, say, the music and film sectors.

With distributors slow, then, to adapt their operations to a variety of cultural and technical changes, there exists a significant opportunity to launch web-based alternatives more in tune with producers' needs. Using Mute's own thirteen years of experiences as a starting point, NDS prioritises the creation of online communication, fulfilment, tracking and payment systems which fit in with the ways that cultural outfits are known to actually operate. It integrates these into a social-network style structure which also fosters a sense of community.

Practicalities, Business Model

The system works by creating a global web of locally-inputted information, ranging from producers and agents (resellers) to outlets and cultural goods. The recruitment of 'agents' is essential for the system as it is these site members' intimate knowledge of their respective locales that enables the product to reach new audiences.

Agents transport or sell on the products in question in exchange for a commission on sales. The integration of web-based international payment systems (primarily PayPal), mechanisms for ad-hoc price setting, postal and courier fulfilment support these core exchanges – together with all the tools routinely available on social networking sites, such as trust/quality rating, etc.

Users engage with NDS in the following ways:

- *Upload contacts*
- *Add their cultural goods/media*
- *Recruit people to distribute and sell goods/media*
- *Organise events to promote the system and its use*

Two core barriers to the creation of a global market place for independent cultural products are high freight costs and a parity of goods' prices. We are tackling these through what we (and others) call:

- *'Community Couriering' (CC) – where people carry goods for less than commercial couriers' rates (when they are taking certain routes for other purposes already)*
- *Peer-to-Peer E-commerce (P2P EC) – where producers and buyers negotiate prices to index them to the purchasing power in the relevant region rather than via a straight currency conversion (this is known as Purchasing Power Parity[1]*

NDS's business model is to take a small commission on each sale and transport transaction, as well as offer advertising opportunities and licence versions of the site technology to particular sectors, agencies or member networks. This income will underpin the maintenance, support and service functions to make it a viable – and reliable – resource over the longer term. Consultancy with core project partners and ongoing solicitation of user feedback aims to ensure the platform can adapt – not only to users' various needs, but also to the complexities of local conditions as they exist on the ground. It is very clear that the multiplicity of documentation work being made by individual artists, the agencies and institutions which service them, as well as a host of other intermediary organisations, is not reaching the full audience that it might – especially not internationally. We believe that NDS can improve this exposure for the UK cultural sector and foster cultural exchange more generally. Successful bids to launch a Dutch-language sister project (funded by Kennisland.nl), and a calendaring subcomponent (funded by the Open Society Institute), suggests the platform's solutions to these long-standing problems resonates with the zeitgeist. With a version of the project tailored to the 'Global South' being pitched to the Ford Foundation simultaneous to one at Arts Council of England, national UK level, we feel we have the kind of broad-based plan in place that can deliver our aims.

Why Mute Publishing?

Mute's diversification into the provision of web and consultancy services is now nearly five years old. Projects like NDS are all part and parcel of the 'do it yourself' approach to media driving the magazine itself, and thus a logical step in the evolution of our organisation as a whole. All the large-scale technology projects we have initiated, notably web tools provider OpenMute (which has a user base of approximately 1000 and has now expanded into Print On Demand consultancy) are aimed at broadening access among the cultural and 'independent' sector to new, sophisticated web and software tools, and sharing lessons that we have learnt pushing the magazine into new formats and environments with a broader community of producers. Distribution has been one of our longest-standing challenges and keeps NDS close to our hearts. The project has the unique distinction of being as useful to ourselves as to others, as well as offering a platform from which to launch the numerous books we are midwifing through our Print On Demand services (April 2008). In talks, workshops and presentations we've done on the proposed system, we have already received interest from many other cultural and magazine networks (for example, Transmission, Mag-Net Electronic Culture Publishers, Documenta Magazines and Eurozine.com).

5NDS started life as an in-house project nearly three years ago. Mute Publishing has conducted extensive research and development and approached its partnerships with care – often discussing the project with collaborators for several years. In the intervening period, much has changed (including the very public explosion of the Web 2.0 phenomenon), but the collective assessment of the project's usefulness remains unchanged (it is ironic that it has taken quite as long as it has for some very simple ideas to find credence via slogans such as Chris Anderson's 'the long tail', but NDS nonetheless illustrates it extremely well).

Notes

[1] http://en.wikipedia.org/wiki/Purchasing_power_parity

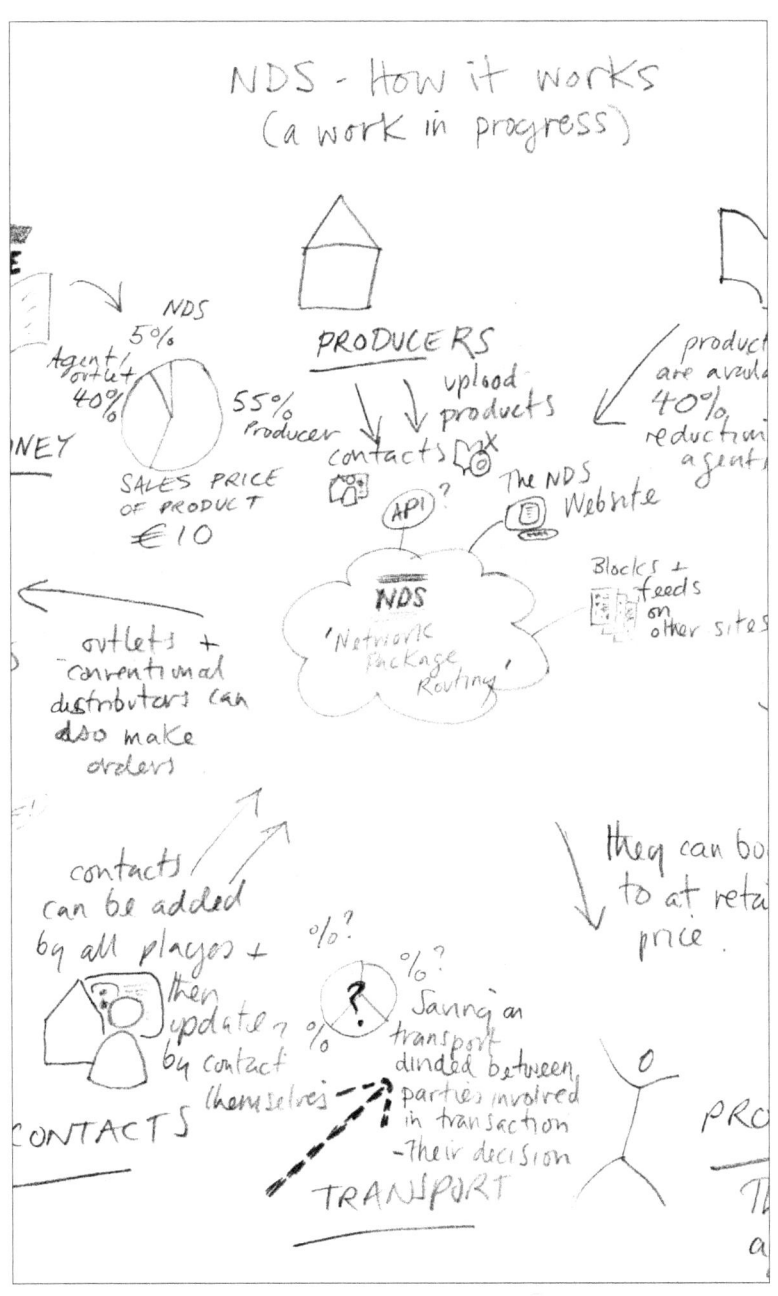

Awkward Gestures: Designing with Free Software

Open Source Publishing (OSP) is a Brussels-based design team that uses Free Libre and Open Source Software (FLOSS), open fonts and copyleft licences for its productions. We aim to make our designs available as source material whenever possible and try to persuade our clients to do the same.

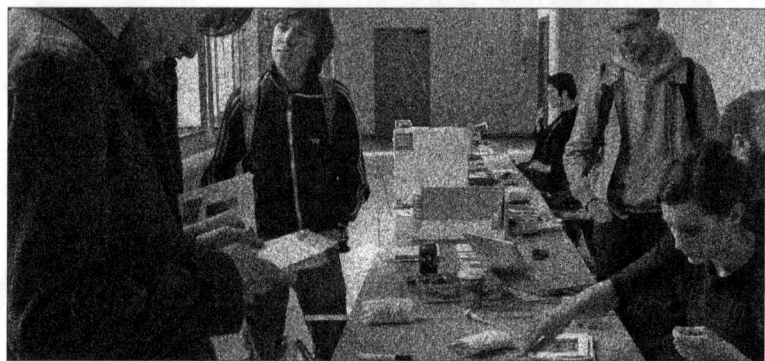

Print Party avant la lettre: production line for an 'exquisite corpse' publication as part of <u>The Tomorrow Book Project</u> (Jan van Eyck Academie, Maastricht, 2006)

We launched OSP because our portfolio started to fill up with designs for alternative music, copyleft activities and Linux Install Parties. The gap between the language of our work and the jargon of the commercial software we used became more obvious with every new job. We were also interested in the role that software plays in the creative process and trying to find out how our digital tools could become a creative and substantial element in design itself. But since the software packages of Adobe Inc. have become quite the standard in art academies, creative studios and print shops, it is difficult to detect their influence, let alone analyse their effect.

Over the past two years, OSP has created a number of publications, posters, brochures and websites with Free Software and this experience has changed our practice. Although this was clearly our objective, it also led to surprising discoveries about the way we work and what we actually expect from software.

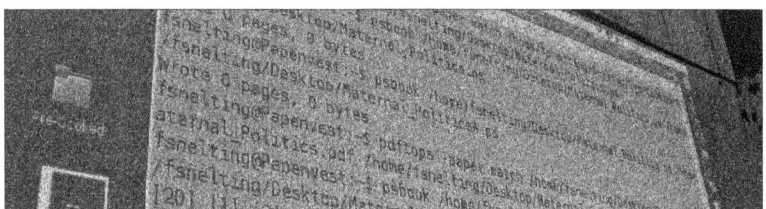

Print Party 0.2: How To Print A Booklet in 19 Easy Steps; the projected command line interface shows the second last step (Interface 3, Brussels, 2006)

Almost every poster, website or publication that is created nowadays is the result of a partial or a complete digital process, but worldwide there is just one single company that supplies designers with the tools to make them. Adobe's out-of-the-box packages are certainly powerful, but since they can only be customised superficially, the wish to 'make a difference' starts to become an argument to choose a more active engagement with software. It has even led to the acknowledgement of Open Source as an option, most notably by the Adobe company itself. Design critic David Womack compares it to the production of the T-Ford[1]. Although a streamlined process might be faster, it runs the risk of everything looking the same in the end. Thus, in order to make your mark, a diversification of tools is necessary.

With the production of the T-Ford, that of course had much more to do with the fact that, from then on, cars looked more or less identical; software does not merely determine the boundaries of visual expression. Because it is constantly present, it conditions our practice in terms of division of labour, vocabulary and the physical relationship with the digital medium. Our choice for a different toolset is therefore as much related to ethical considerations as it is to aesthetic considerations; OSP is first and foremost an attempt to facilitate a design practice that starts from a critical use of technology and explicitly functions in an ecology of knowledge based on distribution and circulation rather than competition and exclusion.

Mastering your tools

At the end of the 19th century, machines increasingly took over the work of typographers, printers and typesetters. Designer and socialist William Morris was convinced that workers should not only have collective ownership of their own means of production, he also believed in another form of 'mastery', i.e. the skilful employment of techniques and materials[2]. For Morris, there was more to it than just being handy; his Arts and Crafts movement brought together artists and designers who thoroughly reflected upon the influence of the production process on the nature and meaning of everyday objects. For them, getting the job right implied not only the economic ownership of machines and resources, but also the technical mastery of the work instead of being the machine's slave. Designer David Reinfurt observes that the over-determined functionality and staggering complexity of professional design software makes users restrict ourselves to standard techniques and tools[3]. How could Free Software be more empowering? The fundamental difference it makes is that it allows us to use, analyse, change and distribute source code. In a sense, users literally get hold of their means of production. But while a computer programmer can feel in control by having the right to adjust software, every other 'power user' with the same rights, is practically blown away by the explosion of procedures, formats and processes they are confronted with. Let alone the fact that the 'means of production' for designers include more than their software[4], our experience of designing with Free Software has shown us over and over again that 'owning' our tools is not the same as 'mastering' them.

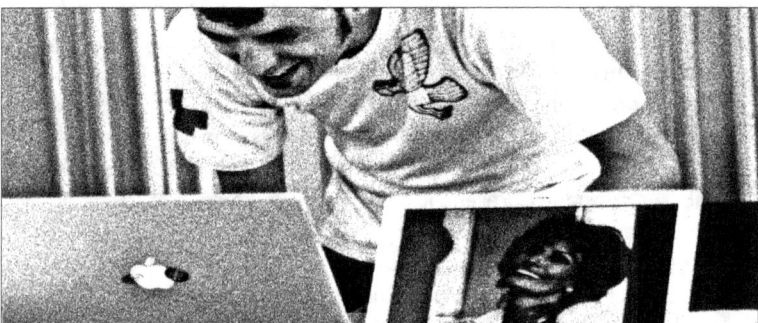

Print Party 2.0: Sophia Loren, "All you see I owe to spaghetti" (Quarantaine, Brussels, 2006)

In Design by numbers[5], the book that led to the development of Processing, a visual programming language that has become popular among designers, John Maeda warns that a clever use of software is often wrongfully considered as craftsmanship. His point is clear; unless we learn to use code as a material, we will never become the master of our software. A comparable argument can be found in the enthusiasm for the command line interface, as this facilitates communication with the numerical operations of the machine itself. Without detracting from the thrilling experience of effortlessly commanding the shell or self-confidently manipulating squares and circles in Processing, we need to avoid a tunnel vision of technology where practices, conditions and perspectives can and must be pushed aside to enable a sense of control.

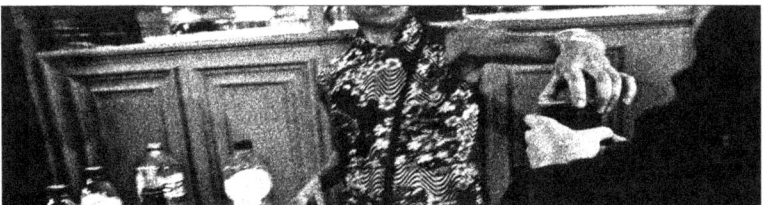

Print Party 2.0: Kate Rich presents the Cube Cola reverse engineering project, serving Cuba Libre *(Quarantaine, Brussels, 2006)*

By cutting a comfortably coherent slice out of the unruly entity that is software, you might miss the opportunity to engage with it in other ways than as a means to an end. Software is source code, but also an interface that, whether graphic or not, represents a particular interaction with the underlying processes. Groups of users gather around certain applications and thereby create patterns of use that make sense of this interaction. Mailing lists and documentation on software are characterised by a specific language and tone, as is the way software developers converse with each other and their users. When we consider software as culture, it is perhaps possible to drop the rhetoric of master and slave, and we can begin to think about how 'competence' can mean more than 'control'.

Making an account of itself

In The Confessions of Zeno,[6] Italo Svevo describes how one evening Zeno strikes up a conversation with a doctor who explains to him at length how 54 muscles are in motion when you walk rapidly. Zeno becomes fascinated by this extraordinary account of the monstrous machinery of his own body, but his curiosity proves to be fatal: *"Of course I could not distinguish all its fifty-four parts, but I discovered something terrifically complicated which seemed to get out of order directly I began thinking about it. I limped, leaving that café; and I went on limping for several days."* From that moment on he is unable to think about this memorable evening, the doctor or even about his own legs without starting to stagger. Is a similar principle at work in software? Apple promotes its operating system with *'software that just works'* (apparently you don't need to worry about it at all). And Adobe makes every effort to push the simulations and algorithms, the monstrous machinery that defines the software, into the background. Recognisable patterns are inventively arranged in well-organised and reliable interfaces, minimising their own presence and creating a feeling of naturalness. Free Software on the contrary categorically refuses to disappear out of sight, if only because it's not mainstream. Simply by offering an alternative, it already makes a statement about itself and, without even making a spectacular difference, certain automatic actions that otherwise would have remained unnoticed become visible.

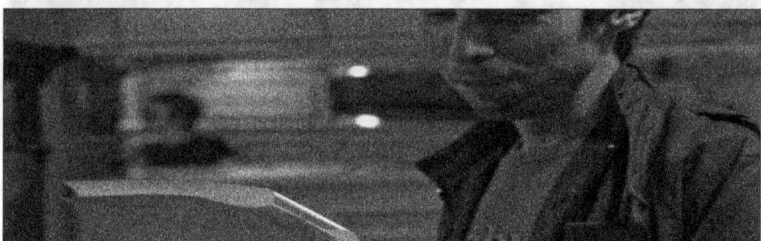

Print Party 2.0: Each of the 19 steps is carefully followed from the paper recipe (Quarantaine, Brussels, 2006)

It could also be a side effect of the Linux/Unix philosophy itself, where the emphasis is on small specific tools that are good at executing relatively simple and well-defined tasks with the intention of giving users as much freedom as possible in order to let them compose their own more complex configurations later. The software remains tangible, because the same recognisable elements can be connected to each other again and again in many different ways. With this modular structure of clearly defined 'clutches' in the form of pipes and standard streams (stdin and stdout), the shift from one action to another is easy to experience. And once you get to know this versatile set of tools a little better, you will detect their traces everywhere, even in more complex graphic applications.

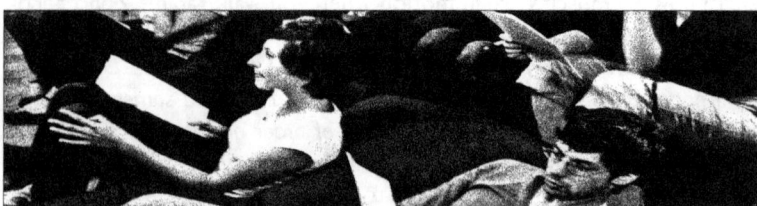

Print Party 2.0: The 19 commands that we typed one by one into the terminal caused a funny yet fascinating spectacle that ended only when 16 pages were correctly printed, folded and stapled together (Quarantaine, Brussels, 2006)

The generative principle that characterises FLOSS has led to an incredible variety of programmes; in graphic interfaces alone there are numerous differences. A volunteering developers' community is less motivated to hide their efforts from users (the identity of the project actually matters) so the convergence of tools that we are accustomed to from Adobe and Apple is less likely to happen. This can be clearly experienced when working through the differences between Scribus (desktop publishing), Gimp (image editing) and Inkscape (vector graphics editor), three programmes that OSP often employs side-by-side. Whether it's the result of a lack of attention or the outcome of deliberate choices, moving between these programmes reveals the culture of its developers, its technical construction and development history. At times this can be destabilising but more often it is inspiring, as it constantly reminds us of the cultural aspect of software production.

Matthew Fuller introduced the term interrogibility[7] to describe the quality of software to make an account of itself and to share the premises on which it is based with its users. It is important how well something can be put to use for a specific purpose, but also to what extent it clarifies the processes that it generates. It is here where FLOSS can make a difference. By considering interrogability beyond the obvious level of source code, software opens up to be used in different ways than intended, even as a tool to think with.

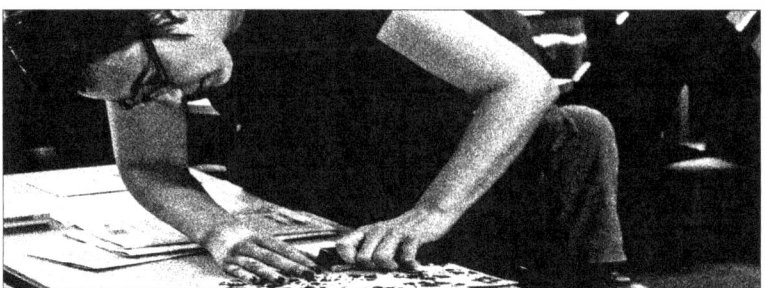

Canadian Printing Breakfast: travel report of a visit to the Libre Graphics Meeting in Montreal (Nepomuk, Brussels, 2007)

"A sane person", says Zeno, "doesn't analyse himself, doesn't look in the mirror"[8], just like software is only noticed when it doesn't work. When a hammer is broken, you realise how heavy and how big it actually is, how its weight is relative to your own strength and how its size relates to what you actually wanted to do with it.[9] Also proprietary programmes have their bugs and glitches, but it is the automatic reflex of FLOSS developers not to avoid or hide them. On the contrary, it is important that imperfections remain visible so that users feel inspired to report them or do something about them.

The obligatory use of open standards is the last but not least reason for processes being more explicit in FLOSS. Far from being normalised, they often cause obstructions in the publishing workflow where documents are sent back and forth between authors, designers and printers. The risk of a possible incompatibility compels us to warn, to explain and to be alert during each moment of the process. Conversions are never flawless.

Awkward gestures

Not unlike Zeno's experience, it is difficult to stay in motion when the machinery comes to the fore. Anyone who has seen a designer at work knows that the self-assured agility with which a layout is done or how the tension of a digital curve is determined, leaves little or no room for questions about the nature of the underlying processes. Taking doubt into account implies breaking with the natural 'flow' of things and accepting the hitches that aren't always that easy to deal with. It is in this way that we have started to understand the importance of performing our practice publicly because it brings out unusual gestures that break with the appeasing elegance of the typical self-assured designer who has everything sorted.

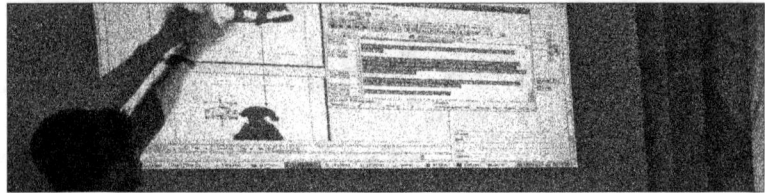

Canadian Printing Breakfast: Turning a frog into a prince and back. Scribus meets Python (Nepomuk, Brussels, 2007)

While a familiar gesture is one that fits perfectly well in a generally accepted model, an awkward gesture is a movement that is not completely synchronic. It's not a counter-movement, nor a break from the norm; it doesn't exist outside of the pattern, nor completely in it. Just as a moiré effect reveals the presence of a grid, awkward behaviour can lead to a state of increased awareness; a form of productive insecurity that presents us with openings that help understand the complex interaction between skills, tools and medium. The Print parties that we organise now and then in a vacant café, a bookstore or a classroom are irregular public appearances whenever we feel the need to report on what we discovered and where we've been; as anti-heroes of our own adventures we keep contact with our fellow designers who are interested in our journey into the exotic territory of BoF, Version Control and GPL3[10]. We make a point of presenting each time a new experiment, of producing something printed and also something edible on site; it is the tension between those parallel processes that defines those infectious events. Throughout our practice we are looking for forms of reflection that can do without comfortable distance. We use our awkwardness as a strategy to cause interference, to create pivotal moments between falling and moving, an awkward in-between that makes space for thinking without preventing us from acting.

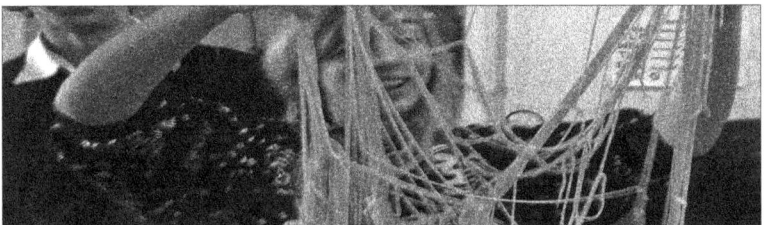

Free Operations: design students produce, cook and eat pasta while we talk to them about Free, Libre and Open Source Software (Werkplaats Typografie, Arnhem, 2007)

Notes

[1] Steven Heller en David Womack. Becoming a Digital Designer, A Guide to Careers in Web, Video, Broadcast, Game and Animation Design. John Wiley & Sons, 2007.
[2] *"It is not this or that... machine which we want to get rid of, but the great intangible machine of commercial tyranny which oppresses the lives of all of us."* William Morris. Art and Its Producers, and The Arts and Crafts of To-day: Two Addresses Delivered Before the National Association for the Advancement of Art. Longmans & Co., London, 1901.
[3] David Reinfurt. Making do and getting by. Software and design. Adobe Design Center Think Tank. http://www.adobe.com/designcenter/thinktank/makingdo (March 2008).
[4] See also: Why you should own the beer company you design for (interview with Dmytri Kleiner). http://ospublish.constantvzw.org/?p=380, 2007
[5] John Maeda. Design By Numbers. The MIT Press , 2001.
[6] Italo Svevo. De bekentenissen van Zeno. Athenaeum-Polak & Van Gennep, 2000.
[7] Matthew Fuller. Softness. Interrogability, general intellect; art methodologies in software. Media Research Centre, Huddersfield, 2006.
[8] Svevo. 2000
[9] Sarah Ahmed. Queer Phenomenology: Orientations, Objects, Others. Durham and London: Duke University Press, 2006.
[10] BoF: Birds of a Feather, informal meetings based on shared interest. Version Control: system to track changes in software development. GPL3: fiercely debated update of the General Public License, now explicitly excluding Digtial Rights Management.

152: A Book itself is a
little machine;

158: Although print remains
indispensable, it no longer seems
indispensable: that is its curious
condition in the late age of print.

259: Possessed of two minds: my own
and its augmented silicon.

276: No text has meaning alone. All
texts have meaning in relation to
other texts.

259: Print is a content, not the
form, of electronic media.

221: The book is an increasingly
obsolete form of communication.

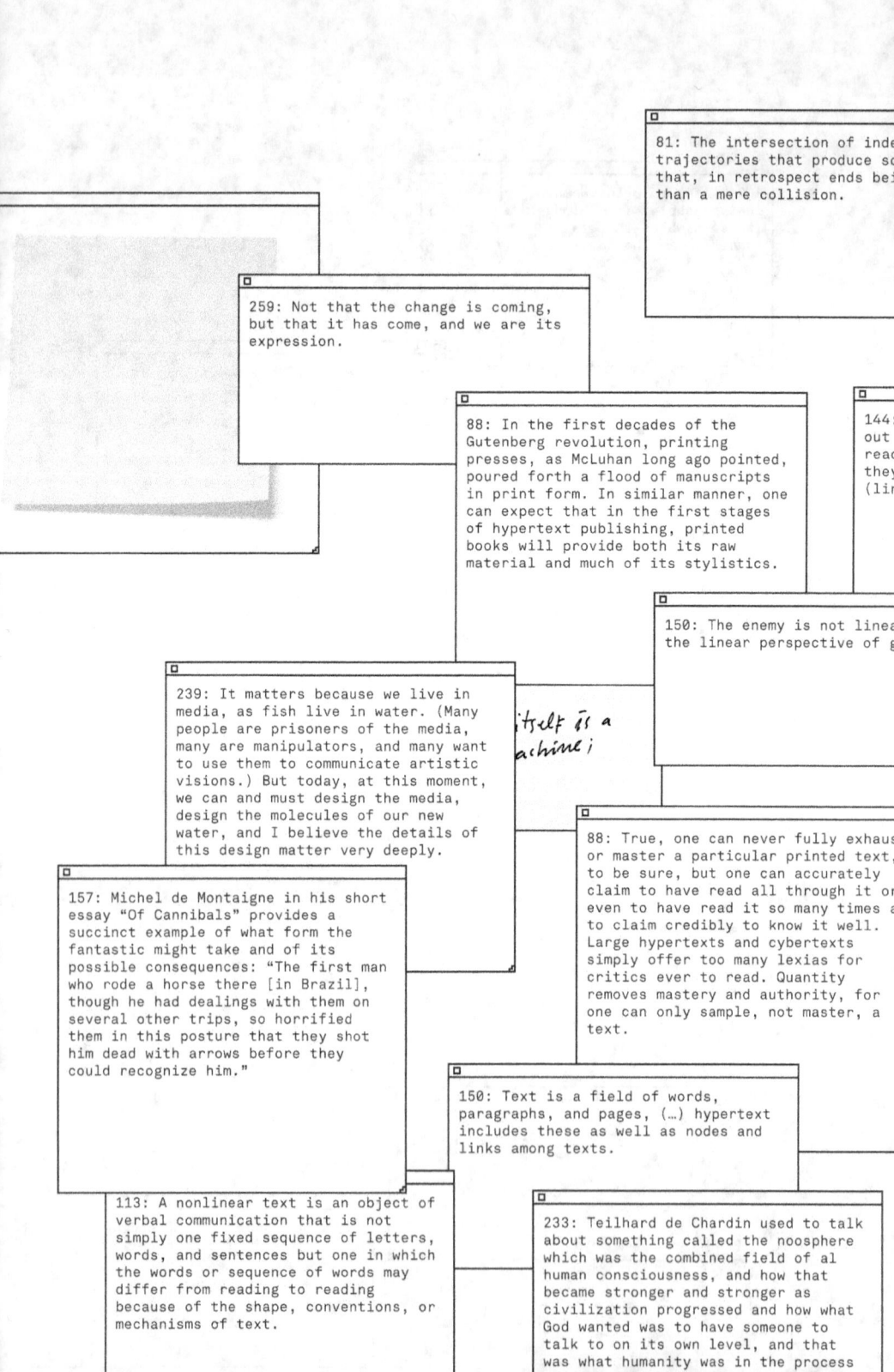

81: The intersection of indep
trajectories that produce som
that, in retrospect ends beir
than a mere collision.

259: Not that the change is coming,
but that it has come, and we are its
expression.

88: In the first decades of the
Gutenberg revolution, printing
presses, as McLuhan long ago pointed,
poured forth a flood of manuscripts
in print form. In similar manner, one
can expect that in the first stages
of hypertext publishing, printed
books will provide both its raw
material and much of its stylistics.

144:
out a
reade
they
(line

150: The enemy is not linear
the linear perspective of ge

239: It matters because we live in
media, as fish live in water. (Many
people are prisoners of the media,
many are manipulators, and many want
to use them to communicate artistic
visions.) But today, at this moment,
we can and must design the media,
design the molecules of our new
water, and I believe the details of
this design matter very deeply.

itself is a
achine;

88: True, one can never fully exhaust
or master a particular printed text,
to be sure, but one can accurately
claim to have read all through it or
even to have read it so many times as
to claim credibly to know it well.
Large hypertexts and cybertexts
simply offer too many lexias for
critics ever to read. Quantity
removes mastery and authority, for
one can only sample, not master, a
text.

157: Michel de Montaigne in his short
essay "Of Cannibals" provides a
succinct example of what form the
fantastic might take and of its
possible consequences: "The first man
who rode a horse there [in Brazil],
though he had dealings with them on
several other trips, so horrified
them in this posture that they shot
him dead with arrows before they
could recognize him."

150: Text is a field of words,
paragraphs, and pages, (…) hypertext
includes these as well as nodes and
links among texts.

113: A nonlinear text is an object of
verbal communication that is not
simply one fixed sequence of letters,
words, and sentences but one in which
the words or sequence of words may
differ from reading to reading
because of the shape, conventions, or
mechanisms of text.

233: Teilhard de Chardin used to talk
about something called the noosphere
which was the combined field of al
human consciousness, and how that
became stronger and stronger as
civilization progressed and how what
God wanted was to have someone to
talk to on its own level, and that
was what humanity was in the process
of creating. That comes as close as I
can to describing what I think is

153: In a written text, the letters of the alphabet are distinct and relatively stable; attempts to show the play of unity and disunity in a text do not (normally) need to question the identity of the letters that compose it. The form of the text is in the paragraphs and sections. So, too, the form of the hypertext will be in the links and paths, not in the individual units.

158: Although print remains indispensable, it no longer seems indispensable; that is its curious c

126: Content is recast in metaphors of mathematical information. In fact, the decisions about what constitutes a textual or visual element actually restrict these content containers to a temporal or spatial unit (the sentence, the paragraph, the photo-graph) that reinforces traditional assumptions about language, meaning, and design.

ally, text is n
ted. Rather, t
d attention sh
lly drawn from
another.

113: When a system is sufficientl complex, it will, by intention, fault, or coincidence, inevitably produce results that could not be predicted even by the system designer.

158: In the late age of print, however, we are concerned not that there is too much in our minds to get down on paper, but rather that there is too much information held in electronic media for our minds to assimilate. We are now overwhelmed from without rather than from within.

158: the Web has provided the most convincing evidence of the computer's potential to refashion the practice of writing.

: The exchange process follows the
r profile perceived by the
chine. When a c
machine, it
ans
ect
pr
fil choice or
ces increasing
lic these diff
into new
fully expl
programmab

276: No text
texts have m
other texts.

113: When you read from a cybertext, you are constantly reminded of inaccesible strategies and paths not taken, voices not heard. Each decision will make some parts of the text more, and others less, accesible, and you may never know the exact results of your choices; that is, exactly what you missed. This is very different from the ambiguities of a linear text.

165: As de
drawn to

243: Computing is not about computers any more. It is about living.

6: If words are always contextual
d contested, then the introduction
static images, hot links, sound
les, animation, and video raises
e stakes exponentially by challeng-
g the underlying metaphors of
formation that are invoked in most
scussions of multimedia.

221:
obsol

88: Collage, or collage-like effects, in fact appear inevitable in hyper-text environments, and they also take various forms. Including blocks of nonfictional text or images within a hypertext fiction, as we have seen, provides one way that such collage occurs; it also happens when authors write and, one might say, along with texts by others.

253: - ACCESS TO COMPUTERS OUGHT

Ghosted Publics – the 'Unacknowledged Collective' in the Contemporary Transformation of the Circulation of Ideas

Andrew Murphie

*'I thought I had reached port; but I seemed to be cast back again
into the open sea'*
(Deleuze and Guattari, after Leibniz)

Ghosted Publics

Publishing has always ghosted the 'public'. It is only a question of the manner of haunting. As with many ghosts, however, in the past publishing as a process (as opposed to the contents published) has tended to be seen, only occasionally, out of the corner of one's eye. It has been conveniently ignored the rest of the time by most people, with the exception of 'experts, specialists and professionals'.

That all this has now changed is well known. Everyone is now a publisher. Indeed, we are all increasingly forced to publish, whether in refereed academic journals or on Facebook. The crises that have arisen are many: about the nature of the new forms of haunting; about which publics are haunted by which new forms of publishing and vice versa; and about who gets to be the publicly validated expert, specialist or professional (the 'journalist', the 'academic', the 'activist', the 'intellectual', the 'artist'). Most importantly, perhaps, the opening up of the processes of publishing has led to a series of institutional crises (in universities, in newspapers and other in mainstream media, in museums, in the sciences and in political organisational forms as basic as the party).

Here I will briefly sketch a series of ideas that unashamedly attempt to describe some general principles by which to approach the contemporary state of 'publishing'. I am particularly concerned with publishing's relation to what I am calling the *'unacknowledged collective'* that I see as crucial to the transformation of the circulation of ideas.

The Unacknowledged Collective

Contemporary publishing in general, in concept as well as in practice, is perhaps in a similar position to music some time ago. By this I mean the period during which music was poised between sampling and scratch's initial opening up of music production, and the later development of mp3s and file-sharing that opened up music distribution. In the case of music, sampling and scratch had turned everything on its head even before the mp3. Likewise, *the transformation of publishing has already occurred.* What is left is the playing out of this transformation in all its complexity. As this transformation occurs, in an ongoing evolution of publishing's forms of production and distribution, what will happen to social practices, art practices, institutions and new forms of collectivity? They will perhaps form that which I am calling an ongoing '*unacknowledged collectivity*'. This is the ongoing processual collective that is ghosted by, and in turn ghosts, contemporary networked publishing's processes and evolutions. It is 'unacknowledged' in part because it cannot be seen or pinned down. Knowledge of an unacknowledged collectivity is at best partial. Members can influence it anonymously, without direct presence. They can be a part of such collectives without knowing each other, without knowing even the extent of otherness involved, without in fact knowing they are part of a collectivity at all in anything more than a vague sense.

The unacknowledged collective, then, inhabits the technical processes of publishing themselves, and it is only these processes that fully register this collective's gestures and movements. At the same time, this collective is a process that is never quite a finished assemblage, because it is always moved by the contingency of contexts, or the resonance of a transversal connection. It is of course never visible in its entirety. Always differentiating itself from itself, it creates a perpetual 'molecular revolution' across techno-social orders, as Félix Guattari put it. Those readers/users moved by the gestures and signals of contemporary publishing are immersed in the mist of unacknowledged collectivity, without finding its ground.

From another perspective, unacknowledged collectivity is also unacknowledged because traditional institutional forms do not often acknowledge these new forms of collectivity, for the obvious reason that they cannot afford to do so. Unacknowledged collectivity haunts these institutions with their undoing. If institutions do acknowledge the new forms of collectivity, it means acknowledging radical change.

In what follows I will begin with academic publishing – the acknowledged collective – and soon open this out to wider considerations of the unacknowledged collective that now haunts all forms of social life.

The Exhausted Academy on the Digital High Seas

I am personally very fond of academic publishing of all kinds – commercial and otherwise. In addition, I think we live in an unprecedented golden age of publishing. Despite this, however, there is a futility to some of the signals academic publishing attempts to send out today. Academic publishing often seems to signal that it is 'waving, not drowning' in the new digital high seas. In fact the fear of drowning is very real indeed. Much of this fear concerns the collapse of authority.

The academy and its acknowledged collectives, most importantly commercial publishing houses, have multiplied, fully capitalised, and even automated the technical processes – such as article refereeing – that affirm the authority of the intellectual. Or, rather, as the intellectual after all exists outside the academy as well as within, what has been affirmed through these processes is the *particular authority of the institutions of knowledge*. Of course, this often excludes the amateur, the un-institutionalised activist, intellectual or artist. This is a technical expansion with regard to so-called 'cognitive capital' at the junction of institutions and markets. Sometimes it seems that little remains free or open if it can be helped – that the free and open should be bought off if it can, and brought into the sanctioned circuits between institutions and markets. For those already in the institutions, or trying to gain access to them, the expanded market for publishing has meant a *command* to publish (or, famously, to perish), and to do so more often, with sanctioned journals or commercial publishers. This command extends not only to employed academics, but to those without work, or employed only precariously. In fact, it extends increasingly to others, to artists, or even politicians.

There have, of course, been many forms of resistance. For example, blogger and academic Danah Boyd recently called for a boycott of locked-down academic journals, while the Public Library of Science's Richard Smith accused traditional commercial publishers of academic material of acting like slave owners. He sees open access advocates as abolitionists. More positive events have included the rise of publishing organisations such as the Public Library of Science, and, more recently, the Open Humanities Press.

Yet most of this is before one gets to the fateful meeting of acknowledged collectivities with the unacknowledged collectivities in which they are increasingly immersed. In this situation, as every publisher or even blogger knows, it's sink or swim. Taking everything and everyone it can on board as it tries to tame the unacknowledged collective, academic publishing is both fully extended and rapidly exhausting itself. At the same time, the gestures of authority it performs are faltering – as they are in the music industry, traditional journalism and the museum. Much of this is to the good, but not all. In *Zero Comments*, media activist (and academic) Geert Lovink understands blogging, in its diminishing of authority as leading to a culture based of nihilism. This leaves a vacuum that, for example, provides an opening to well-funded and tightly coordinated programmes of misinformation in critical areas such as global warming. Even an organisation of some 11,000 plus scientists recognised by the United Nations, the Intergovernmental Panel on Climate Change, is not safe.

As I suggested above, the transformations behind such instabilities have already occurred. All individual events and processes of publishing, including those sanctioned by institutions and markets, are now being swamped by the diversity of means, acts and availabilities of new forms of publishing. Even if we want to, it is perhaps not possible to defend the traditional values or authority of the academy, the newspaper, or the art museum. It is rather time to re-evaluate cultural values from within the more contingent and diverse contexts of contemporary social needs and processes.

Five principles by which this might begin to be done:

1. Publishing is now a generative, recursive network of events, with multiple forms of feedback into the ongoing mutation of forms of publishing themselves.

2. There are an increasing number of bifurcations in publication architectures, at the same time as transversal connections disrupting boundaries between traditional areas. These concurrent splits and transversal connection come together into something resembling an algorithm for artificial life. Publishing becomes a processual programming that generates something like an expanding, evolving artificial 'life of the mind'. Except that this is not artificial. Or, as always, the division between artificial and not makes less sense.

3. Ecological contaminations between all forms of publishing are rife, so that publishing is now a kind of 'chaosmos', a dynamic, complex, if only partially organised chaos. Finance, labour, security, accreditation, circulation, authority, even social action and meaning, in becoming published, are all mixed up. This is the new groundless ground underneath the blurring of institutional, commercial, intellectual and creative work. So when we think about the processes of publishing, we need to think how the process itself constantly evolves, has itself become contingent, not only how content has become more contingent because of new processes of publishing.

4. The life of the mind is not a creative industry. It is a struggle, as always, with creative industry, if using the tools and contexts provided in part by that industry.

5. We are not, despite everything, done with hierarchies. In fact, the likelihood is that the loss of the means of affirming authority – closed refereed journals, highly structured relations between institutions, artists and intellectuals – might only mean that more pernicious means of affirming authority may arise.

In the light of these principles, I present first a kind of loose manifesto for a horizontal life of the mind, followed by a description of a few of the more disruptive ghosts surrounding this new life.

23 Theses for a Horizontal Life of the Mind

1. The new life of the mind found in publishing is founded upon a molecular revolution in technical process and collectivity, *one which can be chosen, but cannot be escaped.*

2. Contemporary publishing is *focused increasingly upon the processes and impacts of publishing itself, rather than content.* This is not to say content does not matter. It does, but a consideration of content needs to be put to one side if we are to understand contemporary publishing, the unacknowledged collectives it brings into being, and only then perhaps the impact and exchange of ideas.

3. The speed of publishing – and the modes of feedback into the mutating processes of publishing – now fragment the act of reading and readership. This 'fractalises' both the life of the mind and collectivity. It does so down to physical, or more specifically *proprioceptive-cognitive engage-*

ment (carrying a book, sharing a conversation, multi-tasking in front of the computer screen). The way this engagement is configured at a proprioceptive-cognitive level is critical to intellectual life, if often forgotten. (Fractalisation describes the 'texture' of 'intermediate temporalities' in life as lived, or the fractal effect of mixing temporalities in 'becoming' [Guattari, *Cartographies Schizoanalytiques*, p219]).

4. This changes the nature of all forms of publishing, especially as they attempt to reconstitute the social or communal. Forms of contestation multiply but are also subject to white anting almost before they get going. Activism itself is therefore made even more processual – unending. As in the fight against corporate interests concerning global warming, *the processes of publication surrounding political events are like gardens that must be constantly tended.*

5. On the other hand, *this only makes the inherent processual nature of activism more obvious*, and therefore makes activism more effective.

6. Whilst control by protocols, passwords and the idiosyncratic tailoring of web response to individual users has been massively increased, *accreditation is collapsing as a form of certitude.* Accreditation has been the founding stone for nearly all forms of authority that involve publishing – from journalism to the purchase of degrees in universities, and of course publishing itself. Even within activist debates, again such as those surrounding global warming, the collapse of an accreditation is feeding into a kind of flattening of structures of authority.

7. We are perhaps approaching – as a community – the state of that which Jacques Rancière calls 'the ignorant schoolmaster'. The focus on process means that we no longer need to know something ourselves in order to make learning possible for others. *The hope is for a true – and not just symbolic – series of gestures towards democracy or real equality.* But much is at stake. Rancière also writes about a 'hatred of democracy' that arises with more virulence in the contemporary world (and which of course makes good use of new forms of publishing).

8. *Publishing should be defined as broadly as possible*, almost to the boundaries of life and culture. Consider the publication of genomic material, or, via increasingly sophisticated brain scanners, of the electro-chemical activity of the brain.

9. *Culture has trouble dealing with, but nevertheless primarily is, currently, the processual proliferation and shift in the processes and definition of 'publishing'.*

10. None of this implies that the power of 'the book' is diminishing. In fact, as with the song in the early days of file-sharing for music, the book is currently getting out of control, in pdf-sharing and in the book's hesitant but inevitable liberation from its material form. Of course, we will still have the physical book, but only when we want to.

11. *Publishing is no longer a question of 'readership' but of resonance.* Only lazy, old media add up the numbers of individuals who look at what they publish, and leave their audience research at that. More astute contemporary publishing focuses on resonance and the shifting of forces within unacknowledged collectives and technical networks. The blogger Larval Subjects advises us to think 'about rain drops in a pond', as 'the waves these drops produce converge and diverge with one another producing additional patterns'.

12. What are the publishing equivalents of music's scratch and sampling? The publishing equivalent to scratch is the attention to the granular within publishing techniques – from the digital breakdown of typographies and colour, to the coding, breakdown and new flexibility of technical processes, along with reader/user behaviours. All of these can be processually reformed *ad infinitum*. The publishing equivalent to sampling is the heart of publishing as it has always been - recording and copying - except that now publishing processes are as so much more diverse in structure, enabling both new forms of recording and copying, and new forms of translation between these.

13. If the printing press was publishing's first trip into orbit, digital publishing is the beginning of the exploration of the virtuality of McLuhan's 'Gutenberg Galaxy', its relational potential.

14. This exploration is also an absorption of other galaxies into the unacknowledged collective. Optical Character Recognition, for example, is only one aspect of a massive expansion of forms of recognition that are in fact a form of reproduction and distribution tailored to *publishing* *as the implosion of galaxies into the Gutenberg.* A voice, a face, a genome recognised – in process – is one that can instantly be 'published', as is a style, a theme, an idea (I don't mean the reductive form of Dawkins' 'meme' here). All of these can be transformed by each other in the publishing process. (Sometimes at odds with their institutions, but sometimes not – for example, MIT – there are an increasing number of intellectuals within and outside of the academy engaged in the interlinking of all forms of publishing. One beautiful example is the browser-based reference plug-in, Zotero, which will soon enable transversal research connections by unacknowledged collectives.)

15. The so-called 'semantic web' is not a neatly ordered set of dictionary-like protocols. It is a universe (and a meta-verse) in constant transition. The semantic web is a far too limited concept for all that can be networked, in process, indeed in constant collision.

16. What are needed are not only the tools to manage these collisions (even as they make them occur). We also need to *work towards redefining the concept of publishing itself, because this concept is an important technical component of publishing, in so far as it folds back into publishing processes.*

17. There is already a generic 'reader' – it is called a computer.

18. Publishing has long been subservient in thinking culture to writing, to culture, to 'works'. Things are now, for the time being, inverted.

19. *Publishing is now ongoing work.* Nothing is simply 'published'.

20. Publishing should not be overly attached to the academy, even though it might sometimes be funded by the academy. It should be free and open. There might be a need for commercial book publishing, which currently produces as good and as diverse a range of publications as one could imagine, although what the future is here is clouded. There is no longer a need for the commercial publishing of academic journals.

21. There is, ironically, *little full freedom within publishing, even of the best kind, because publishing is about responsiveness to unacknowledged and shadowy collectives.* It is also often compulsive; in fact, it represents a new sort of compulsive behaviour at individual and collective levels. This is also why no one should be forced to publish (except for the case below).

22. What might be forced to be published would include *all research in science, even if it fails.* This applies not only to the academy, but to commercial research.

23. Free speech is important but it's not enough. *Free expression now includes access to complex networks of resonance.*

Disruptive Ghosts
Finally, some disruptive ghosts that haunt ghosted publics should be mentioned.
The first of these is the open itself. Open publishing is open to everyone. Large companies, for example, can serve their own interests via publishing (again climate change is a case in point). Openness is only the beginning of the good. It is also, of course, never completely open. Ned Rossiter characterises the problem as one of *networked organizations versus organized networks.*

Then there is the simultaneous expansion and collapse of expertise. Anyone can be an expert today, although the more so if they can find funding from some think tank or other. Yet, to once again return to the example of global warming, sometimes accredited expertise – some kind of authority – is a necessity. The question then is whether a new kind of authority without hierarchy is possible. If such a thing is possible, it will be made so by new forms of publishing and new ghosted publics. This much is well known, if still an unsolved problem. Key to this problem is the need for *adaptive forms of expertise, along with criteria for evaluation of the forms of expertise needed in specific ecologies of publication/unacknowledged collectivity.*

Despite such problems, new publishing processes and unacknowledged collectivities must find relations that are mutually beneficial, and sustainable in relation to other ecologies. If publishing has become as critical an issue as I have suggested here, this sustainability is perhaps more important than is often allowed in thinking about contemporary media and the social.

Contributors and Acknowledgements

Biographies.

ARTELEKU (ES)
Is an interdisciplinary arts centre offering both theoretical and practical activities. It is a centre that is permanently expanding and constantly changing, open to growth and knowledge. Arteleku provides support for art that produces and promotes a wide variety of concepts, that can be disseminated externally, and in turn also reflects (on) our society, public and community. Arteleku is supported by the Gipuzkoa Provincial Council of Cultural Promotion and Diffusion Department.
http://www.arteleku.net/

Canal Contemporâneo (BR)
Achives and spreads information, knowledge and debate about Brazilian contemporary art through its different online modules. Based on the concepts of Virtual Community (Rheingold), Radical Media (Downing) and Tactical Media (Garcia/Lovink), it has been efficient in rousing communication and interaction, connecting people and institutions around the 27 Brazilian states and over 80 countries. Its activism guides journal articles and has encouraged political mobilization, like for example the inclusion of Digital Art in Brazilian cultural funding policies (2004). Canal Contemporâneo took part in exhibitions such as hiPer> relações eletro // digitais (hiPer>electro//digital relations), curated by Daniela Bousso (Santander Cultural, Porto Alegre, Brazil), Tudo aquilo que escapa (Everything that escapes), curated by Cristiana Tejo (Museu do Estado, Recife, Brazil), Ocupação, (Paço das Artes, São Paulo, Brazil) and has also taken part in the Documenta 12 Magazines initiative. Since 2006, the special projects of Canal Contemporâneo have been sponsored by Petrobras, Brazil's major cultural sponsor.
http://www.canalcontemporaneo.art.br/

Patricia Canetti (BR)
Multimedia artist, born in 1960, lives and works between Rio de Janeiro and São Paulo, Brazil. She is the initiator and moderator of Canal Contemporâneo, a digital community focusing on Brazilian contemporary art. Together with Canal, Canetti takes part in exhibitions and coordinates several projects and events, like "Fórum Conexões Tecnológicas", which was held by Sergio Motta Art and Technology Award, and the Documenta 12 Magazines' initiative. Since 2005, she has been a member of the Prix Ars Electronica International Advisory Board of Digital Communities.

Miguel Carvalhais (PT)
Born in 1974, lives and works in Porto, Portugal. He lectures at the Design Department of the University of Porto (FBAUP), where he is currently developing a PhD dissertation on the study of creative practices in procedural systems. He has worked as a communication designer, and founded and directed the rev-

design studio (1997-2004). He currently heads the design laboratory of FBAUP. As a musician, he collaborated with several artists and performers, a.o. developing the @c project with Pedro Tudela and Lia (2000). He co-founded the Crónica media label (2003-), which he still runs.
http://www.carvalhais.org
http://www.cronicaelectronica.org/
http://www.at-c.org/

CONSTANT (BE)
Is a non-profit association, based and active in Brussels since 1997 in the fields of feminism, copyright alternatives and working through networks. Constant develops radio, electronic music and database projects, by means of migrating from cultural work to work places and back again.
http://www.constantvzw.org/

Régine Debatty (BE/DE)
Writes about the intersection between art, design and technology on her blog we-make-money-not-art.com as well as on several design and art magazines such as Art Review (UK) and a minima (SP). She also curates art shows and lectures internationally.
http://www.we-make-money-not-art.com/

Leandro de Paula (BR)
Born in 1982, lives in Rio de Janeiro, Brazil. He graduated from the Universidade Federal Fluminense in Cultural and Arts Management. He is currently studying for a Masters in Communication Studies at the PUC-Rio. With Canal Contemporâneo, he took part in Documenta 12 Magazines as content editor.

Jaime Iregui (CO)
Is an artist and the editor of [esferapública]. Along with other artists he founded independent spaces of exhibition and discussion such as Magma (1985-87), Gaula (1990-91), Tándem (1993-98) and Espacio Vacío (1997-2003). He is currently Associate Professor of the Department of Art at the Universidad de los Andes.
http://esferapublica.org/

Christina McPhee (US)
Is a native of Los Angeles. She earned and MFA at Boston University in painting, following a BFA from Kansas City Art Institute and studies at Scripps College, Claremont. She teaches in the Film and Digital Media Department at the University of California-Santa Cruz. She has been a moderator for the -empyre-network, since 2002 and was a participating editor in the Documenta 12 Magazine Project (2006-2007)..Engages a psycho-geography of environmental risk and traumatic memory in layered, baroque visual and media suites. Her photography and video work has been shown internationally, a.o. at the Bucharest

Biennial, Itaù Cultural, the Whitney Museum of American Art (Artport), and many others. Her writing and net art appear with Turbulence, VIROSE, CTheory, Neural, Drunkenboat, and Soundtoys. She created video sets for Pamela Z's electronic solo opera, "Wunderkabinet". She has been a visiting artist /fellow at Bauhaus University Weimar, Banff Center for the Arts, and Vermont Studio Center, and has performed and presented at a.o. the ICA, London, Royal Academy of Architecture Copenhagen, Royal Melbourne Institute of Technology (for DAC), Futuresonic Manchester, and FILE (Sao Paulo).

http://christinamcphee.net
http://www.subtle.net/empyre

Nasrin Tabatabai & Babak Afrassiabi (IR/NL)

Are artists living in Rotterdam and working both in Tehran & Rotterdam. Beside their individual artistic practises, they initiated together the project Pages in 2004, which offers critical views on art, culture, urbanism and social issues. While Pages constantly searches for ways to surpass predefined and geographically bound discourses of subjectivity and locality, through its projects it tries to examine the possibilities within interaction and juxtaposition of various local discourses that may condition a space of critique or moments of critical practices. Since 2004 they produced 6 issues of a bilingual Persian/ English magazine, as well as a number of collaborative projects that have been introduced in different exhibitions and presentations. They have participated a.o. in the Documenta 12 magazine project (2007), the 27th Sao Paulo Biennale (2006), Interrupted histories. Ljubljana, SI: Museum of Modern Art (2006), the 2nd International Biennial of Contemporary Art of Seville (2006), On difference #1. Local contexts - hybrid spaces, Stuttgart, DE: Württembergischer Kunstverein (2005), Collective creativity. An exhibition on collective practices & group enjoyment. Kassel, DE: Kunsthalle Fridericianum (2005), the 3rd Tirana Biennial. Tirana, AL (2005), News from Tehran 1. Rotterdam, NL: Witte de With (2004), Recreation. Nantes, FR: Musée des Beaux-Arts de Nantes (2004).

http://www.pagesproject.net

Alessandro Ludovico (IT)

Is a media critic and editor in chief of Neural magazine from 1993, (Honorary Mention, Prix Ars Electronica 2004). He is the author of: 'Virtual Reality Handbook' (1992), 'Internet Underground.Guide' (1995), 'Suoni Futuri Digitali' (Future Digital Sounds, 2000) and co-edited the 'Mag.Net Reader' series (2006–). He's one of the founding contributors of the Nettime community and one of the founders of the 'Mag.Net (Electronic Cultural Publishers organization. He also served as an advisor for the Documenta 12's Magazine Project. He teaches at the Academy of Art in Carrara. With Ubermorgen and P.Cirio he developed 'Google Will Eat Itself' (Honorary Mention Prix Ars Electronica 2005, Rhizome Commission 2005, nomination Prix Transmediale 2006) and 'Amazon Noir' (1st prize Stuttgarter Filmwinter 2007, Honorary Mention Share Prize 2007, 2nd

prize Transmediale08) art projects.
http://neural.it
http://magnet-ecp.org

Nat Muller (NL)

Is an independent curator and critic based (mostly) in Rotterdam. She has held positions as staff curator at V2_, Institute for Unstable Media (Rotterdam) and De Balie, Centre for Culture and Politics (Amsterdam). Her main interests include: the intersections of aesthetics, media and politics; visual culture, (new) media and art in the Middle East. She has published articles in off- and online media; is a regular contributor for Springerin and Bidoun, and has given presentations on the subject of (new) media art (inter)nationally. She has curated video screenings for projects and festivals in a.o. Amsterdam, Rotterdam, Berlin, New York, Istanbul, Copenhagen, Grimstad, Dubai, Lugano and Beirut. Recent collaborative projects include The Trans_European Picnic - The Art and Media of Accession (Novi Sad, 2004), DEAF_04: Affective Turbulence: The Art of Open Systems (Rotterdam, 2004); DEAF07 (Rotterdam, 2007), Visual Foreign Correspondents (Amsterdam 2007-8). Other projects include a.o. INFRA_ctures (Rotterdam, 2005), Xeno_Sonic: a series of experimental sound performances from the Middle East (Amsterdam, 2005), the workshop 'Between a Rock and a Hard Place? (Amman, 2007). Together with Alessandro Ludovico she is editor of Mag.net Reader2: Between Paper and Pixel (2007) She has taught at the Willem de Kooning Academy (NL), ALBA (Beirut), the Lebanese American University (Beirut) and the American University of Dubai (UAE). She is curator-in-residence at the Townhouse Gallery in Cairo from April 2008 to April 2009.
http://www.labforculture.org/en/labforculture/blogs/10739

Andrew Murphie (AUS)

Andrew Murphie is the editor of the open access, online journal, the Fibreculture Journal and Associate Professor in the School of English, Media and Performing Arts, University of New South Wales, Australia. He works on: theories of the virtual; post-connectionist and poststructuralist models of mind; Guattari and Deleuze (and others - he's not quite a card carrying 'deleuzean'); art and interaction; electronic music (especially in Australia); critical approaches to performance systems and what he calls 'auditland'; biophilosophy and biopolitics; innovation; education and techology; contemporary publishing. Recent online publications include 'Differential Life, Perception and the Nervous Elements: Whitehead, Bergson and Virno on the Technics of Living' in Culture Machine (2005) and 'The Mutation of "Cognition" and the Fracturing of Modernity' in Scan (2005). He very occasionally pretends to be an amateur VJ, as VJ Comfy, and sometimes works with the wonderful Senselab in Montréal.
http://senselab.erinmanning.lunarpages.net/web-content/
http://www.andrewmurphie.org/blog/
http://journal.fibreculture.org/

Jelena Vesic (RS)

Is an independent curator, art critic and editor who lives and works in Belgrade. She is also co-editor of Prelom Journal and member of the Prelom Collective She graduated from the Art History Department, Faculty of Philosophy - Belgrade. She also attended the School For History and Theory of Images – Belgrade, and the Curatorial Training Program in De Appel – Amsterdam. Her work is mostly dedicated to the politics of representation in art and visual culture, as well as critical examination of new models of interaction between theory and art in the broader social field. Her curatorial practice often experiments with frameworks, methodologies, contextual and collaborative aspects of the presentation of art. She has published her texts in various art magazines, readers, catalogues, books, journals and art blogs. She participated in numerous panels, symposiums and discussions related to the issues of curatorial work, education, publishing and criticism.

http://www.prelomkolektiv.org

Simon Worthington (UK)

Is co-director and co-founder of the cyberculture magazine Mute and Mute organisation, London, and has been involved in various projects with the latter. In addition he is co-founder of 'Mag.Net (Electronic Cultural Publishers organization).

http://www.metamute.org

Acknowledgements

The editors would like to thank all contributing authors for sharing their ideas and thoughts in this project. "Another culture is possible—not impossible! A conversation between Fran Ilich and Cornelia Sollfrank", is kindly reprinted here in abbreviated version, and first appeared on [http://www.thing-hamburg.de/index.php?id=654]. Without the financial support of LabforCulture.org and arteleku, in particular the efforts of respectively Angela Plohman and Miren Eraso, this publication would have remained a mere idea. Georg Schöllhammer, who directed the Documenta12 Magazines project, initially brought most of us together in July 2007 for the Paper&Pixel Debates, and thus can be credited for planting the first seed of this project.